ONE OF 'THE FEW'

ONE OF 'THE FEW'

*Describing the experiences of Ted 'Shippy'
Shipman, who called his part in the
Battle of Britain 'my gentle battle'*

By

John Shipman

Pen & Sword
AVIATION

First published in Great Britain in 2008 by
Pen and Sword Aviation
an imprint of
Pen & Sword Books Ltd
47 Church Street
Barnsley
South Yorkshire
S70 2AS

ISBN 978-1-84415-687-0

Typeset in 11/13 Palatino by
Concept, Huddersfield, West Yorkshire

Printed and bound in England by
CPI UK

Pen & Sword Books Ltd incorporates the Imprints of Pen & Sword
Aviation, Pen & Sword Maritime, Pen & Sword Military, Wharncliffe
Local History, Pen & Sword Select, Pen & Sword Military Classics
and Leo Cooper.

For a complete list of Pen & Sword titles please contact
PEN & SWORD BOOKS LIMITED
47 Church Street, Barnsley, South Yorkshire, S70 2AS, England
E-mail: enquiries@pen-and-sword.co.uk
Website: www.pen-and-sword.co.uk

This book is dedicated to all the men and women who took part in the Battle of Britain in the air and on the ground, and especially those who were killed in action.

Contents

Preface

It has been a pleasure, an honour and a big learning experience to compile this book, which originated from some notes, a typed text (which was not originally intended for publication) and a collection of carefully labelled photographs and other artefacts left to me by my father. I have decided to retain the style of the original text but I have taken the liberty of adding some further notes and pieces of information which I hope will help to complete the picture. The reader will remember that these are Ted 'Shippy' Shipman's notes which describe his experiences during the early part of the Second World War and the crucial Battle of Britain and afterwards in the Cold War and then up to retirement.

The notes that were used as a basis for this book were written in the 1970s with the intention of recording some of the events in the Royal Air Force which might be of interest to others in the future. Ted Shipman was not the type of man to spin a yarn or to impress people with stories of wartime exploits and other achievements. He preferred to reflect on the past and in his modest way think that sometime in the future these notes might shed some light on how life used to be. Ted Shipman was not one to force his ideas or experiences on other people, and he was for ever mindful that to young people the past might be boring or not wholly relevant. His far-sightedness to record many recollections, with prompting and encouragement, has enabled the reader to benefit from these experiences. Quietly, over the months, Ted penned his notes in longhand, and finally the notes were typed up by Margaret Shipman.

Much later, in 2006 and 2007, the notes were married up with some relevant pictures and additional information in order to compile the text you now see. Ted Shipman's plain, no-nonsense narrative style has been retained and left as it was as much as possible.

JMS
2008

Acknowledgements

Special thanks go to Margaret Shipman for typing the first text from Ted's longhand notes. Individual pictures and drawings are credited thus [ ] where known. Endnotes identify the source of material and provide further information.

Additional material has been provided from a number of sources, and thanks go to the following persons in particular:

Bill Norman
Chris Goss
Dan Johnson
Eleanor Collins
Hans Kettling
Norman Spence
Philip Harvey
R.W. 'Wally' Wallens
Steve Brew

My apologies to anyone who has contributed material or information and has not been fully credited.

Further information may be obtained from John Shipman,
3 Old Mill Close, Langford, Biggleswade,
Bedfordshire SG18 9QY. Tel: 01462 700650

Introduction

When I left my father's farm in 1930 to enlist in the Royal Air Force as an aircraftsman second class (AC2) for eight years it could not be foreseen that I would serve almost thirty years in the RAF. Neither would it be imagined that I would fly for thirteen years as a pilot in nearly forty different types of aircraft, achieve the highest grade of a flying instructor and retire as a wing commander decorated with the Air Force Cross. Although my prospects on the farm were poor for economic and family reasons, my decision to go into the Royal Air Force was fostered by my long and increasing interest in aeroplanes and their activities, especially from nearby aerodromes. However, I came to regret that I did not join as an apprentice at Halton, but I didn't, so I missed that opportunity and the benefits it might have offered.

Life in the Royal Air Force was varied, interesting and challenging. Of course there were disappointments but also opportunities to be taken and achievements to attain. I count myself lucky to have served my country in a wide variety of experiences, meeting and working with people of position and character, Royalty, chiefs of staff, commanders-in-chief and many other officers and individuals who made my service the more memorable.

CHAPTER 1

Taking the Plunge: Enlistment

On 26 May 1930 I left home for London and the RAF. Naturally my feelings were mixed, but they improved as time passed. The recollections of West Drayton are few. It was the Reception Centre where the new boys were arriving in ones and twos, a wide cross-section of individuals, two Scots, a Welshman, a lad from Colne in Lancashire, Jim Berry, who was a close friend for years, several Brummies, and 'Dizzy' Baker.

One scene at West Drayton remembered clearly was the attestation, the swearing-in and taking the oath of allegiance. This was done on the Bible, of course. One man, a Jew, did not use the Bible.

THE DEPOT AT UXBRIDGE

After about a week at West Drayton we were bundled into a lorry and taken to the recruit training school at Uxbridge. Fatigues figured prominently in the first few weeks. The worst were potato peeling and washing greasy tins in the airmen's mess. Without exaggeration some of the food at times took some facing, even by a really hungry recruit.

Then came the seemingly endless kit inspections, scrubbing and blancoing of webbing equipment, then sewing on linen tapes showing our official numbers – 512770 for me. Then came the exasperating task of putting on puttees so that they were not too tight nor so loose that they would slip down and come undone. Even so there was the more difficult job of avoiding gaping 'letter boxes' at the back of the leg where the calf narrows towards the ankle. Finally the problem was to arrange the winding of the puttee so that it finished exactly in line with the outer seam of the pantaloon, as the knee breeches were called.

Our instructor was a sergeant (ex-Scots Guards) and an excellent chap whom we liked a lot. The Flight Commander was a flight sergeant named Bishop, who was much less likeable, ruthless and hard, but he had a great reputation for training the RAF guards for the Cenotaph services and for Olympia. On one occasion he made the whole squad, including the instructor, scrub and re-blanco our webbing equipment every day for a week! We did not know why. Rifle drill, marching, physical training and other minor activities made up a continuous programme. Every Sunday brought a church parade for which we marched to and from Uxbridge parish church behind the RAF Central Band. Twenty-four-hour armed guard duty in full pack came round frequently. An instance of Bishop's tough attitude was one day when we were drilling with fixed bayonets and one chap awkwardly and accidentally caught the fellow in front with the point of the bayonet; Bishop's only comment was that he should have given it a bloody good twist before pulling it out.

The training was tough and at times sticky, in more ways than one. The summer was hot and the parade ground had recently been resurfaced with tarmac. We did a lot of square-bashing on the new surface. By the time we had passed out we were fit and more confident young men.

Uxbridge had its legends, and one of these concerned Air-craftsman Shaw, otherwise known as Lawrence of Arabia. It was said that when he went on church parade one day the Sergeant Major noticed that Shaw was not wearing any medals as others of his age were. The Sergeant Major asked if he had any medals, to which Shaw said he had, and he was told to go and put them on. When he returned he was relatively plastered with them. This caused consternation among the officers, which resulted in Shaw being asked to leave the parade.

School of Technical Training for Men at Manston

It was late summer when our squad passed out at Uxbridge, split up and went our different ways for trade training. I had enlisted as a 'Driver, petrol', which was one up from 'Driver, steam'. The distinction was real enough, as both petrol and steam-driven lorries were common at this time. Manston was a flying station as well as a technical training school, and flew two types of aircraft – Vickers Virginia night-bombers and Armstrong Whitworth Atlases used for army co-operation. The aerodrome was a large grass one with an open public road running across part of it. Built during the First World War, Manston was unique in that it originally had underground hangars built under the living quarters part of the camp. Two or three aircraft entrances to the hangars appeared as cuttings going down into the chalky ground on two or three sides of the camp.

First time airborne

Occasionally when the Virginias were night flying I would go down to the hangars to watch them, and on one such occasion my opportunity came for me to have my first-ever flight. It was a clear dark night with little moon, and a sergeant pilot was getting dressed to fly. Plucking up courage I asked him if I could go up. The answer was yes! I was soon installed in the rear cockpit. Although I was wearing my greatcoat I knew that it was going to be cold, but it would be worth the discomfort. I felt strangely remote in the tail cockpit at the rear end of the fuselage and behind the rudders and elevators, which I could easily touch while watching them move to and fro and up and down. This gave a peculiar sense of communication with the pilots far away at the other end of the fuselage. I could see their heads from time to time moving above the rim of the cockpit, and then watching the constantly moving controls provided some satisfaction of being in touch with them. The tail of the aircraft seemed anything but rigid; it shook and twisted in the slipstream of the two propellers, especially during take-off and landing. This trip was, on reflection, quite unique, for apart from it being my first time off the ground, the position of the rear cockpit gave me the beating blasts of hot air from the propellers, seasoned with the unmistakable smell of burnt castor oil. This embellished the experience of watching the whole of the aircraft in front of me, to be a part of it but yet not a part of it.

R101 DISASTER

On the morning of Sunday 5 October 1930 we were roused very early with the order to get ready to leave camp in best blue, which meant breeches and puttees. The airship R101 had crashed in France and we were to stand by to bring the bodies of those who were killed back home. However, after several hours of tense waiting we were told that we would not be needed after all.

Our only participation in this tragedy was to attend a drum-head service on the tarmac in front of the hangar on the day of the funeral of the victims. This was my first experience of such a service, and I found it most impressive. The solemn music of the band, the fresh breeze erratically flapping the ensign's ropes against the flagpole and the billowing of the chaplain's surplice in the otherwise perfectly silent atmosphere of a dead aerodrome during the two minutes silence was most moving. The sounding of reveille finally broke the silence and brought the release of many held-back coughs. Simultaneously, an aeroplane flying very high appropriately helped to bring us back to reality. It is such experiences that remain in the mind for a lifetime.

SCHOOL OF ARMY CO-OPERATION AT OLD SARUM, SALISBURY PLAIN

On 9 January 1931, I was posted to Old Sarum, which was the School of Army Co-operation. The transport section here was largely a pool of drivers and vehicles for the various Army manoeuvres held from time to time. We had some thirty-six drivers but only six or seven drove regularly on the road on routine camp duties. The main purpose of the school was to help in the training of pilots who were learning to 'spot' for the Army, and during each course we used to lay out on the ground in the countryside strips of white oilcloth about ten feet long and one foot wide as symbols representing various formations of Army units. The pilots then had to 'spot' these markers and report back by wireless telegraphy radio or by message-dropping their location, size and number. These exercises were good fun for we left early in the morning with rations for the day, scores of oilcloth strips and maps with lists of secret timed grid references and symbols to display. The area in which we worked extended about thirty miles from the camp, so there was plenty of travelling and quite a lot of planning of routes in order to be at the correct time and site and displaying the right symbol. At times these spotting markers had to be changed and removed according to our instructions.

Two incidents are worth recording. One day we had put out strips in a parallel fashion on a hillside just opposite a farm. Later, when we collected them, the farmer met us and asked us if we were 'dryin' 'em'. Another time, again near a farm, we came back for the strips to find they were gone. Looking around we saw that the farmer had nailed them to the roof of his fowlhouse to repair a leaky roof! These trips were a welcome change to the usual routine and were certainly useful in learning to read a map.

Airborne again

Each year we looked forward to the summer camp of the university air squadrons. This meant much more flying from the aerodrome by Avro 504Ns and a few Bristol Fighters which were being used for training. It was the rule that all the aircraft had to be air tested by the instructors before the pupils were taken up, so there were opportunities for passengers. This was how I got my second flight. The instructors really did test the aircraft, and took the opportunity of crazy flying and letting themselves go. Loops, rolls, spins, stall turns and falling-leaf manoeuvres – quite bewildering, almost frightening. Some passengers were sick, but fortunately not me. Perhaps I was too scared!

Rifle shooting

Old Sarum gave me the opportunity to take up rifle shooting, both small and full bore. There was an excellent indoor range for 0.22 calibre, and we had two teams which competed regularly in Nobel Trophy competitions. These were postal shoots in which target cards were shot at home and against other stations. We had good rifles and great support from the station, so we were keen and also very successful. I managed to get in the 'A' team, in which a 'possible' was the normal for deliberate rate of fire and very few points lost in rapid practices. In 1933 we won all our matches, the final one being against Farnborough. Immediately after this match I was posted to Farnborough and scarcely had time to unpack my kit when I was given a set of cards to shoot against – this time against Old Sarum! Perhaps this was the first time anyone had shot for both teams in the same match. Old Sarum won the competition, but since I had been posted to Farnborough I was deemed to be on the losing side, so I watched the presentation ceremony from the hangar doors.

CHAPTER 2

Trying to Get On

Since arriving at Old Sarum in early 1931 from Manston I had been thinking of ways to improve my position and trade. I was an aircraftsman second class (AC2) driver, petrol, in Group V with pay at three shillings per day with an additional three (old) pence per day driving pay. (This equates to 16.25 pence per day.) My aim was to get training as an engineering or aircraft fitter, which would take me from the lowest to the highest trade group and the best paid at three shillings and six pence per day. Within a few months of arriving at Old Sarum I took the trade test and passed for advancement to aircraftsman first class (AC1), but I could not be reclassified until I had been in the trade for three years.

As there were too many drivers, my next thought was to ask for attachment to the aero-engine workshops to learn the trade there – on the job, as it were. My first and second applications for this were turned down; then, after a reasonable time I put the third application in, telling the Flight Sergeant that if this one was refused I would ask to see the Commanding Officer personally, as is allowed in King's Rules and Regulations. This was in the morning, and by the afternoon I was authorised to be attached to the Engine Repair Section (ERS), and that was the end of my driving in the RAF.

BECOMING AN AERO ENGINE FITTER

On reporting to the workshops I joined a gang of fitters doing complete overhauls on Armstrong Siddeley Jaguar engines, which powered the Armstrong Whitworth Atlases. They were 14-cylinder air-cooled radials. This work suited me down to the

8

ground, and I found it interesting and most rewarding. Within about six months I was working on my own, overhauling the complex Claudel Hobson AVT 70G carburettor of the Jaguar; in fact I had to supervise the newly arrived Halton apprentices in this work. Perhaps I was the only AC2 driver, petrol, in charge of AC1 engine fitters in the RAF.

Exactly a year after leaving the MT section I was sent to West Drayton for a trade test to re-muster to the trade of fitter – aero engines (FAE). The test took a whole week, of which the majority was the practical filing test, as well as the oral and written ones. It was quite a sweat, but I passed.

Our method of changing the phosphor-bronze valve guides in the Jaguar cylinder heads was rather crude. It was to heat up the cylinders in a bath of oil on the blacksmith's hearth, and then, using a hammer and a metal drift, drive the old guides out and the new ones in. On one occasion the oil in the bath caught fire, much to the concern of the WO. After this event, whenever we were using this method he would find an excuse to be away from the workshop. Another of his worries was the running of the engines on the test bed after overhaul. The engines were bolted to a large wooden frame on wheels and lashed to the concrete floor. The whole assembly was housed in an open-ended brick building with wire netting covering the open ends. With the propeller fitted and with the open exhausts, the noise was very loud indeed, and when doing the forty-five-minute full-throttle endurance run the whole contraption shook and strained at the wire lashes. We often wondered what would happen if the lashes gave way.

LEARNING TO FLY

Early in the summer of 1933, a mate, 'Lofty' Barkham, entered a newspaper competition for a test flight at a local flying club at High Post, free tuition being the prize. All to no avail, but the club offered him reduced rates. He enrolled, and on his third visit I went to watch. After the flight the instructor said to me, 'What about you?' I agreed, and was having my first lesson at one pound per hour. The instructor turned out to be a flight commander from the RAF Central Flying School (CFS) at Upavon on leave. He was Flt Lt P. McGregor-Watt, who used to lead the inverted flight at the Hendon air shows. He was said to be one of the best six pilots in the RAF. Unfortunately he was killed as the CO of a Hampden squadron in 1939. The aircraft in which I had my first lesson, on 31 August 1933, was a Spartan (G-AAMB) with a Cirrus engine. Instruction continued in a Robinson Redwing (G-ABMF)[1] with an Armstrong Siddeley Genet engine, and then later a de Havilland Moth with a Cirrus engine.

After twelve dual trips and a total of five and a half hours, Flt Lt McGregor-Watt sent me solo on 14 September. It is difficult to put into words the feeling of being up in the air alone for the first time, but it was most exhilarating. Although I had a great sense of achievement, there was also a feeling of concern not to make a 'bog' of it, for this time there was no one to put me right. In the event all went well, and with much relief I did my one circuit and landed without difficulty. It was a great day and I went back to camp feeling on top of the world. By going solo in five and a half hours I broke the club record, and after completing the compulsory three hours solo and taking the examinations in air law and airmanship I qualified for my pilot's 'A' Licence (No. 5979). The total cost for six and a half hours dual and three hours 55 minutes solo was about twenty-two pounds. The sad thing about 'Lofty' Barkham was that he failed to go solo.

South Farnborough

Early in December 1933 I was posted to South Farnborough Station Flight and to fly with the AOC. Apparently it was his custom to have a fitter to look after his aeroplane, arrange details such as maps and weather forecasts, and to take over in the air as required.

I had a distinctly cool reception and interview with the Flight Commander on arriving in Station Flight. He made it clear that he did not approve of such postings. No one liked him and the AOC refused to give any orders for his aircraft through him. Usually he contacted the Flight Sergeant or sent his driver to me. We were all relieved when a new flight commander took over. Flt Lt F.H. Shales was an ex-test pilot and flying instructor who had flown an aircraft after it was released from beneath the R33 airship. Not only did he do this but he flew back to the belly of the airship and re-hooked his aeroplane to the airship! 'Jimmy' Shales was a gentleman who obviously liked things to go smoothly and easily. He would often come into the hangar (the end 'black shed' nearest to the RAE, which was often later referred to in air show TV commentaries), and he would join us on the tarmac near Cody's famous tree and looking up at the sky would ask us what we thought of it. On one or two occasions when he obviously wanted to fly, we deliberately said we thought the weather was not too good, but the real truth was that we had scrubbed down and polished the aircraft for a forthcoming inspection. Perhaps he realised this point. He was most good natured and would enjoy a joke. Once we played a trick on him which he took in good spirit. We tinned a farthing coin with solder and then soldered it to the head of a drawing pin. This we pressed into the wooden floor just inside the hangar door. It was not long before Jimmy came in for one of his routine walks around. He easily spotted the bright shining 'sixpence', stared at it for a while then stooped and made several attempts to pick it up. After a while he gave up and looked around to see a bunch of grinning airmen. He burst out laughing too. We had four aircraft in Station Flight – two DH Moths and two Hawker Tomtits, of which one was K1785. This Tomtit carried the preceding serial number (K1786) to the one that is today preserved in the Shuttleworth Collection at Old Warden in Bedfordshire. We also had several Hawker Harts and Audaxes which were mainly used for photography by the adjacent school.

FLYING WITH THE AOC

I flew regularly with Air Commodore H.M. Le Marchant Brock[2] in the Tomtit. There were visits to army co-operation squadrons at Old Sarum, Odiham, Manston and Catterick. Places visited in this fashion were Tilshead, Middle Wallop, Friday Wood (Colchester), Leigh (Swindon), Brockworth, Knighton Down, Kingston Deverill and Larkhill. A trip from Farnborough with Air Cdre Le Marchant Brock in June 1934 nearly ended in disaster. We were visiting No. 26 Squadron at Catterick in the Tomtit, and we nearly ran out of fuel. We decided in future that we would refuel en route next time.

The Air Commodore was a real seat-of-the-pants flyer. He was not a fair-weather pilot, and flew in all sorts of conditions. Only once were we beaten by the weather. We took off from Catterick and headed for Grantham (Spittalgate), where we were to refuel.

After about an hour we were over South Yorkshire and ran into dense fog. Not having a radio we turned back and landed at Sherburn in Elmet. A telephone call to Spittalgate showed that fog had cleared there, so after about half an hour we took off again. This time we got to just south of Knaith when we again met thick fog. The AOC said that when he could not see the ground he always turned back, but this time we landed between rows of haycocks near Knaith and close to the river.

One of our visits to Old Sarum was to witness a demonstration of the new 'Rota' auto gyro by Flt Lt Howarth Booth which the school had been given to try out. Naturally there were Army top brass there and it was to be an important occasion. Unfortunately, it did not go well. The wind was gusty and the demonstration was staged close to the tarmac and hangars. During one of the landings, just as the wheels touched the ground a gust of wind blew the aircraft sideways, causing it to topple over, the blades striking the ground with resounding whacks, which brought the event to a disastrous end.

Queen Bees

These were Tiger Moths used as live gunnery targets for the Navy. They were remotely controlled by radio from the ground using a 'push-button' control box. When they were flying from Farnborough a safety pilot was on board. However, most of the flying was controlled by radio, including the take-off and the landing. Owing to the hangars sometimes interfering with the radio, the pilot on the ground would lose control of the aircraft and needed the safety pilot to take over. The Queen Bees were often fitted with floats, and they were catapulted from ships.

Notes

1. G-ABMF was once owned by Will Hay, the famous Music Hall artist, before being purchased for the Wiltshire Flying Club.
2. Air Cdre H.M. Le Marchant Brock CB DSO, died 11 March 1964. Dep. Commandant ROC 1929–45.

CHAPTER 3

To Fly or Not to Fly?

Having by now achieved the exalted status of leading aircrafts-man in the Group I trade of Fitter Aero Engine, I was permitted to apply for a service pilot's course. This I did, and had I not been known to the AOC I would have had to go before him for his recommendation, but in the circumstances I got this automatically and my application went straight to the Commander-in-Chief. This was Sir Arthur Longmore, who was known to be a supporter of Trenchard's apprenticeship scheme, but to such an extent that he automatically ruled out all applicants for pilot's courses who were not ex-apprentices. This meant me, and I was rejected out of hand without even the chance of an interview.

Many months later I reapplied when the political and military situation in Italy under Mussolini triggered a British rearmament and expansion programme. I had my medical, and a week or so later found myself in front of the C-in-C, who was now Sir Robert Brook-Popham. All went well and I was duly accepted subject to a central medical board examination in London. With this successfully passed, I had now to wait for further instructions.

In due course, on 27 January 1936 I was posted to No. 3 Elementary and Reserve Flying Training School at Brough, on the Humber just west of Hull. The school was run by the Blackburn Aircraft Company.[1] The aircraft used were Blackburn B2s with Cirrus engines and side-by-side seating. They were very sturdy aircraft with all-metal fuselages.

There were thirty-two of us on this course at Brough, twenty officers and twelve airmen, and as it was a civilian-operated school we wore civilian clothes and were billeted in private houses locally. Three officers on the course were newly joined and ranked as acting pilot officers; one of them, Arthur 'Pongo' Scarf, won the VC during the Second World War.

I thought it best not to say anything about my private pilot's 'A' licence; even if my instructor had known of it he would still have had to put me through the essential exercises before solo and during the whole course. All went well, and after five hours and forty minutes of dual instruction I went solo. For this 'second' first solo I was not unduly worried except that the aerodrome was rather awkward, oblong in shape, so that one had to take off and land either towards or over the hangars and aircraft manufacturing works which were at one end. The Humber was on the south side and the aerodrome was scarcely wide enough to operate across it.[2]

A SLOW ROLL IN CLOUD

One scary solo trip I had was while doing practice steep turns and aerobatics in cloudy and stormy weather. As I was doing a slow roll I flew into thick cloud when I was just about upside down. It was probably stupid and careless of me, but the cloud generally was not clearly defined and I suppose I was so preoccupied in doing the actual roll that I did not realise that I was entering cloud. Naturally I had some difficulty in getting back to straight and level again. The B2 had only primary instruments and was not equipped with modern ones. It took me some time to sort myself out. No doubt while attempting to complete the roll, which was the proper way, I let the nose of the aircraft drop and the speed began winding up and I was losing height fairly rapidly. Also, I saw that I was turning, so from the small amount of instrument flying that I had done I realised that I was in a spiral descending turn. I managed to keep my head and remembered that I had first to stop the yaw with opposite rudder and then raise the nose to reduce the speed and finally level the wings. This worked, and I came out of the cloud safely. It must have been a big cloud and quite thick. Naturally I was very relieved to see that I was still not far from Brough, with the Humber clearly visible to the south.

A bunt

Just before the course ended my instructor did a 'bunt', an outside half-loop, with me. He didn't warn me he was going to do it and I was not prepared for it. While flying quite slowly he got hold of the stick firmly with both hands and pushed it slowly to the dashboard. The nose of the aircraft went down and the airspeed rose. I was thrown against my harness and my legs left the floor and shot up towards the dashboard. I felt that my head would burst! As we got to the inverted position the 'upward' force (or should it be downward?) lessened and we did a half-roll out – quite an experience for a raw pupil. It did, however, demonstrate the sturdiness of the B2.

No. 9 Service Flying Training School (SFTS) at Thornaby

On 8 April 1936 I arrived at Thornaby near Stockton-on-Tees. The whole of the Brough course made up the first course at Thornaby to start off the newly formed 9 SFTS. The chief flying instructor was Sqn Ldr D'Arcy Greig of the Schneider Trophy team, my flight commander in 'A' Flight was Flt Lt R.C. Jones and my instructor was Sergeant Eddie Womphrey.

Our aircraft at this time were dual-controlled Hawker Harts with Kestrel engines. We lost no time, and at 09.00 hours on 9 April I was airborne with 'Womph'. After three dual trips totalling an hour and a half, two short air tests as a passenger, and a flight commander's test of thirty minutes, I went solo for the usual single circuit and landing. This was above the average to go solo after only two hours dual, including the flight commander's test, and it was the first solo of the school – for whatever that is worth. Apart from a couple of trips in a Tutor and one in an Audax, all the flying on this initial service stage was on the Hart.

Now followed the Advanced Training School (ATS) for squadron flying. I had been asked whether I wished to go on fighters or bombers, and I suppose because the prospects of fighters sounded more attractive than those of bombers, I chose fighters and went into 'C' Flight, finding that I was the only airman on the course to do so. The aircraft we were to fly in 'C' Flight had just arrived from the makers, and were Gloster Gauntlets with Bristol Mercury engines. We should have had Fury Mark Is, but for some un-explained reason they turned out to be Gauntlets. They were really beautiful to fly, and when the initial shock and of course the thrill of flying what was at that time the fastest fighter in the RAF without being given any dual instruction had passed, every moment in them was a great tonic and morale booster. They were most enjoyable aeroplanes.

Steep turns, aerobatics, spinning and front gun practice made up most of the flying in this term, with a three-week air-firing practice camp at RAF Northcoates Fittes[3] with which to end up. Some more examinations in air navigation, armaments recon-naissance, airmanship and maintenance put me in second place with 90%, making an aggregate of 88% and overall top of the course. My assessment as a pilot was now raised to 'well above average' – all of which gained a 'distinguished pass' that was published in the aeronautical press.

There were several incidents at Thornaby. The first was a collision on the ground by two solo Audax aircraft in very strong and gusty wind conditions. The two pupils flying these aero-planes were unhurt. The second was at night when one of the airmen, Gascoigne, was making a solo landing. It was a very dark night and for some reason he got much too low on the approach. He undershot badly and hit the hedge with the undercarriage and overturned. Although trapped in the cockpit for some time he was not badly hurt. Luckily, too, the aircraft did not catch fire. I was on the flare-path with his instructor, and although we were watching the lights approach and we saw them disappear we hardly heard the crash. It took us quite some time to find the aeroplane, as the navigation lights had gone out in the accident.

On another occasion, during the AOC's annual inspection, one of the pupils was putting on a display of simple aerobatics. He started off all right and was doing a series of loops. Unfortunately he seemed to be carried away by his demonstration and allowed himself to get lower and lower until his final loop looked like ending in a dive into the ground! There were groans from almost everyone – it looked impossible for him to get away with it. He obviously saw his predicament and made a desperate effort to pull out – he almost stalled and sank behind and below the level of the trees at the far end of the aerodrome. Everyone waited breathlessly for the inevitable crash, but he just made it and no doubt landed a very frightened and wiser pilot.

The next incident concerned myself when making a 'battle climb' to 16,000 feet in a Gauntlet without oxygen or radio. The weather was not very good, especially as with a breeze off the sea we were getting a lot of smoke from the Billingham and Middlesbrough factories. There was some cloud at 1,000 feet, too. Having climbed up to height over the aerodrome through a lot of smoke haze and broken but considerable cloud, I began to descend. I was flying in a wide left-hand spiral so that I would not be far from the aerodrome, and by the time I had got down to 2,000 feet I could see that the cloud had thickened considerably in the short time I had been flying. Remembering that there was high ground to the south of the aerodrome I decided to go down to 1,000 feet, and if not out of cloud by then I would climb up a little and fly out to sea on a compass heading and descend in an area where I knew I could not fly into the ground. As I was approaching 1,000 feet I could not see a break anywhere, so I followed my plan of flying out to sea. This idea was put to me weeks before by Eddie Womphrey, just in case such conditions arose. I flew north-east for about five minutes and then descended continuously to about 200 feet above the sea. I cleared cloud and turned on to a heading of south-west to find the coast. After a very few minutes I saw cliffs ahead of me, and as I knew that the only cliffs in that area were south of the Tees I turned north up the coast. I almost immediately spotted the Skinningrove Ironworks between Staithes and Saltburn. Continuing up the coast I easily found the mouth of the Tees and turned in to follow the river on the south side, to avoid the transporter bridge and built-up area of Middlesbrough behind the bridge. The aerodrome was easy to find but it was clear that the weather was much worse than when I took off.

This flight taught me a great deal in practical airmanship and encouraged me to develop a technique of mental dead-reckoning which has stood me in good stead many times since. The idea of mental dead-reckoning is to mentally plot your movements and therefore your position throughout a flight in relation to your aerodrome or some other known point.

The last recollection concerns a pre-flight briefing talk given to us by Eddie Womphrey. As essential part of the flying instructor's job is to explain and discuss the exercise to be done in the air with his pupils before the flight, and this is usually done in the crew-room. It saves a lot of time in the air and gives the pupil an opportunity to ask questions in discussion and away from more tense conditions in the air.

On this occasion 'Womph' was explaining how we should restart the engine of an aeroplane if it stopped while doing aerobatics or some other unusual manoeuvre. Using the accepted jargon he explained that 'if you lose your prop you dive steeply to pick it up again'. This puzzled an officer pupil very much and he said, 'Won't that be very difficult?' 'Why?' asked 'Womph'. 'It's rather a small hole in the prop, isn't it?' replied the pupil. He thought that losing your prop was meant literally and that one had to dive and steer the aeroplane to pick up the prop by getting the shaft from the engine into the hole in the base of the prop. Certainly this would be a puzzling task! This story may seem far fetched, but it is true, and the pupil was deadly serious.

Then came the final parade and the award of the pilot's badge, or brevet – the coveted wings! A couple of days later, on 12 October 1936, I was promoted to sergeant and posted to No. 41 Fighter Squadron at Catterick, together with one of the officers – Plt Off R.A. Barton (a Canadian nicknamed 'Butch').

NOTES

1. Operated by the North Sea Aerial and General Transport Co. Ltd, Brough, Hull.
2. On grass aerodromes one can normally take off and land in any direction to obtain the benefit of a headwind, a higher air speed and a lower ground speed.
3. North-east Lincolnshire coast.

CHAPTER 4

No. 41 Squadron, Catterick

At Catterick No. 41 Squadron[1] had not long returned from Khormaksar near Mersa Matruh in North Africa, and was still in the process of getting its Hawker Demons (two-seater fighters) rebuilt and serviceable. They had been shipped back to the UK in crates, and needed much work to be done on them to get rid of the aftermath of desert conditions. The Squadron Commander was Sqn Ldr J.A. Boret, whose son came to the squadron later when we had Spitfires. After WWII Sqn Ldr Boret became Commandant of the Royal Observer Corps, and we met at a conference at Box, near Bath.

'Butch' Barton was posted to 'A' Flight and I to 'B' Flight, with Flt Lt R.V. McIntyre as Flight Commander. It seems appropriate now to explain that fighter squadrons normally had two flights of six aircraft each, 'A' and 'B' Flights, whose identifying colours were red and blue respectively. These colours were often painted on ground equipment, such as trestles, ladders, toolboxes and tail trolleys, and also on the aircraft wheels, propeller bosses and spinners and on the tailfin. Each flight was divided into two sections of three aircraft because this was, for tactical purposes in air fighting, considered to be the most suitable formation size to manoeuvre in formation, and to fight with mutual support for each other, and yet giving the greatest firepower under the circumstances.

The sections in 'A' Flight were known as Red and Yellow sections, and those in 'B' Flight Blue and Green sections. If any more aircraft were available to fly in the squadron they would normally be classed as reserves, and they would be given another colour such as Black. In fact during the early years of WWII, when the Station Commander and any spare pilots would fly spare aircraft, one heard of Black, White and Purple sections.

By mid-November there were sufficient aeroplanes serviceable and tested for me to fly, and after a brief trip in the air-gunner's seat with another sergeant pilot I went solo in the Demon. I had to do five hours solo, with a ballast weight in the rear seat, before taking a passenger.

The Demon was naturally very similar to the Hart and Audax, except that the engine was supercharged and the undercarriage a little more 'bouncy', which made a good, smooth landing more difficult. Flying during the next few months was devoted to general flying practice, map reading, camera gun exercises, formation and trying to get the radio, the TR9 (transmitter/receiver 9), to work efficiently. Tuning was important, for even after having been carefully set up on the ground we found that the setting altered after take-off. Interference was also a problem, especially from the aircraft's electrical equipment. The TR9 was of course a high-frequency (HF) set, and its range was not great. However, I once had a very remarkable result when taxiing a Demon one night. I heard a very clear transmission from another aircraft which I discovered was at Hornchurch in Essex. I answered this transmission and was heard equally well. This of course was due to freak atmospheric conditions.

BATTLE FLIGHT

One of our regular tasks when we had become operational was for each flight to take it in turn to be the duty battle flight for the week. This meant that the flight was to maintain a higher state of preparedness for the period and to carry out a battle climb with six aircraft, fully armed, to operational height, usually between 16,000 and 25,000 feet. An interception on other aircraft would be made with camera gun attacks, then to land, refuel and rearm as quickly as possible. From touch-down to the start-up after refuelling and rearming the exercise would be timed by stop-watch, and this inevitably brought out the competitive spirit to better the times of previous efforts.

SASO CHECK-UPS

At this time 'Daddy' Probyn was a group captain and the senior air staff officer at Headquarters No. 12 Group at Hucknall. His main responsibility was the efficiency of the squadrons, and in this capacity he showed extreme keenness and ingenuity, missing nothing during his inspection of the aircraft and crews. He 'saw through everything', as it were.

One day we were doing our battle flight climb, and while we were airborne a Miles Magister arrived over the aerodrome quite unannounced. It landed, and it was 'Daddy' Probyn who had come to check up on us! Although it was compulsory for every pilot to 'book out' on every flight to another aerodrome and to signal the intended arrival at the destination (in case of being overdue or in an accident), not so 'Daddy', for that would have given the game away.

We did one climb, interception, attack and landed, and the chaps got stuck into the refuelling and rearming, as usual being determined to put up a good show. Our Flight Sergeant, 'Dusty' Coleman, was there with his stopwatch when Daddy walked past. Daddy said, 'How's it going, Flight Sergeant?' 'Very well, Sir,' replied Dusty, 'I am keeping a check on the time', showing the Group Captain his stopwatch. With a twinkle in his eyes 'Daddy' Probyn quickly held up his own stopwatch and replied, 'Yes, and so am I!'

When we had all started the engines again, the Group Captain signalled to us to switch off, and then he said, 'Now we will see if it has been done properly', and he proceeded to check every fuel tank, gun, ammunition magazine and oxygen bottle. Needless to say, he found one or two blunders.

After lunch it was a tour of the hangars, and the Group Captain walked straight to one of the young pilot officers and said, 'You fly these aircraft and no doubt you help refuel them from time to time; show me where you put the fuel in!' The young pilot promptly pointed to the coolant tank filler cap! 'You don't know much about the fuel system, do you? You had better learn it!' said 'Daddy' Probyn. Then he said he would check on the bomb racks of one aircraft, so some dummy practice bombs were loaded up and the wireless NCO who was responsible jumped into the cockpit, saying, 'Right, Sir! I'll release them when you are ready.' 'No you won't, Flight Sergeant, I'll do it myself!' said 'Daddy'.

Some months later, when on another visit, 'Daddy' Probyn was walking into the hangar and past a group of pilots. As he passed them he turned to the one who had boobed on the fuel system previously and said, 'Do you know your fuel system yet?' 'Yes, Sir', replied the young pilot officer eagerly. 'Right', said the Group Captain, 'We'll go into the crew room and you can draw it on the blackboard!' As it happened, all went well.

I always found this alert, sharp-shooting attitude far more acceptable than the easygoing variety. It kept everyone on their toes and produced an efficiency which made for a happy and satisfied atmosphere. The same goes for a good standard of sensible discipline.

NICKNAMES

It seemed natural and very popular to call people by their nicknames, and from the description above Sgt Coleman got the nickname of 'Dusty'. Another popular nickname was 'Lofty', and so was 'Chalky'. It was about this time that I acquired the nickname of 'Shippy'. This stuck all through my service career until I retired.

NIGHT-FLYING

The training syllabus for fighter pilots at Thornaby did not provide night-flying instruction. So I arrived at Catterick completely untrained in night-flying, which was a squadron requirement. There weren't any dual-controlled aircraft in the squadron, so it was a case of 'having a bash'. The usual practice for all new pilots, even if they were night trained, was to do dusk landings, which meant that they started landing on the flare-path in near-daylight, and continued to do landings through the dusk period until it was dark.

One evening in May 1937 I was to do my 'dusk landings'. The flare-path was laid out and lit. We used rather large paraffin Money[2] flares, which were bee-skep-shaped wire baskets filled with asbestos and soaked in paraffin and standing in a tray. Off I went in almost broad daylight. I turned downwind for my first approach and signalled for permission to land, by means of my downward identification lamp. I was given a 'red' light, which meant 'do not land – go around' instead of the expected 'green' from the flare-path controller. Round and round I went asking for permission to land – but no luck – they had decided to change the direction of the flare-path! It was a laborious job, dowsing the flares, loading them onto a lorry, putting them out in the new direction and relighting them. In the meantime it was getting quite dark. Finally I was given a 'green' on the Aldis lamp and made my first 'dusk' landing in almost real darkness. I was the only one flying at the time, and it took me one hour and ten minutes to do five 'dusk' landings. This was certainly a case of being thrown in at the deep end and learning the hard way. Anyway, all went well, and in fact I got to like night-flying and enjoyed it – well, most of it, at least!

Empire Air Day

In these pre-war days we used to put on various demonstrations for Empire Day to entertain the public. There was squadron formation flying, front and rear gun firing using blank ammunition, high- and low-level dive-bombing with smoke bombs and individual aerobatics. No. 26 Army Co-operation Squadron, with whom we shared Catterick, showed off its techniques, too, one of which was message picking up.

Squadron formation flying was the most arduous, especially as a junior pilot in the squadron. The worst position to fly was as No. 12, for in echelon one was flying at the end of a long line of aircraft which tended to whiplash if the station keeping was not steady. It can be a real sweat trying to keep in position in turns, for if you are on the inside of the turn you are flying so slowly that you are almost stalling, and on the other hand, if you are on the outside of the turn, you are usually flying all out. In both cases you have less manoeuvrability than any other member of the formation. Bumpy conditions, of course, make the situation worse, and at the end of a flight one's arms and legs ache like mad.

Bombing, on the other hand, especially low level from 800 feet, was good fun. The technique for accuracy was to half roll into an almost vertical dive on the target, starting with as low a speed as possible and then pulling out at about 150 to 200 feet. By this method one could get within a few yards of the target. High-level dive-bombing from 5,000 feet or more was of course less exciting and less accurate.

SEARCHING FOR CRASHED AIRCRAFT

Catterick is low lying between the Cleveland Hills at over 1,000 feet to the east and the Pennines at well over 2,000 feet to the west. On more than one occasion we had to search the Pennines for aircraft that were reported missing. The weather was usually bad, and with low cloud and rain the Pennines were somewhat awesome and one had to be careful not to become a casualty by getting trapped in one of the steep-sided and narrow valleys. It is remarkable how quickly the clouds can drop down onto the hills, and one can never be sure what conditions will be like from moment to moment over the peaks. I don't remember any of our searches being successful, for the area of search was usually extensive, and it can be extraordinarily difficult to see a wrecked aeroplane unless it is lying very exposed. However, we had to try on these occasions.

INSTRUMENT FLYING

Early in June 1937 I was selected to go with another sergeant pilot, Jimmy Sayers, to Northolt for a 'blind-flying' test with 'Baldy' Donaldson, then a flight lieutenant, who was later to achieve a world speed record in a Meteor, as a group captain. Later, in the 1960s, as a retired air commodore, he became air correspondent with the *Daily Telegraph*. Apparently, a blind-flying, or instrument-flying, instructor was to be appointed for the squadron. We both flew with 'Baldy' in a Tiger Moth and then returned home. In the outcome I was selected, and for the next two and a half years acted as a supervising instructor to the other pilots while they flew on instruments 'under the hood'.[3] The aircraft we used were a Hawker Hart and an Avro Tutor for a while, but later and mainly it was a Miles Magister. I was also appointed a Link Trainer[4] instructor, and in this work devised a series of exercises to practise operation control and interceptions in this trainer. They were also very useful for new pilots to learn and practise radio procedures.

Practice camps

Each year, usually in the summer, we would move the whole squadron to a coastal armament practice camp, where we would fire live ammunition and drop live 10 lb practice bombs. In 1937 we went to Catfoss in Yorkshire, and the next year it was to Aldergrove in Northern Ireland, where we used Loch Neagh as a target area, but this was after we had been re-equipped with Hawker Furies. At Catfoss, with the Demons, we fired front and rear guns on ground targets set up on the sands, and dive-bombing on floating targets in the sea, high level from 5,000 feet and low level from 800 feet. During this camp at Catfoss I dropped sixty-seven bombs with a best score of 22 yards average from 5,000 feet. Then there was air-to-air firing on sleeve and 'flag' targets towed by other aircraft. My air-gunner at that time was a corporal wireless operator who was a complaining sort of chap, and perhaps to excuse his low score one day said his Lewis gun would not fire properly. As a result he was told to take his gun to the twenty-five yard range for test. The resident civilian armourer took the gun, put a pan of ammunition on it and literally played a tune on it! Bang-bang bang bang bang bang-bang bang! The corporal was left speechless and we had no more complaints.

Towards the end of October 1937 we exchanged our Demons for the Hawker Fury Mark IIs, sometimes called Super Furies, with a squadron based at Tangmere, very much to that squadron's disgust and our pleasure. The Furies were wonderful aircraft compared with the Demons, of course, even better than the Gloster Gauntlets we had at Thornaby. They looked very smart with their slick lines and shining cowlings and wheel spats. They handled beautifully, too, and were quite exhilarating to fly, especially when doing aerobatics. The crackle of the open stubby exhausts when throttling back for a landing was a well-known characteristic.

Cathode ray direction-finding tests

Just five days after flying the Fury for the first time I was asked to go to Leconfield to do a test on a new cathode ray direction-finding equipment which had just been produced by the RAE at Farnborough. Apparently the bomber boys from Leconfield gave it a bad report, so we were called in. The weather was bad, with low cloud and rain, and I was forced to fly most of the way at well below 500 feet above sea level, which meant real low flying over the higher ground. The test was very successful, as was that for the return trip to Catterick the next day. Early in 1938 I did two more tests for this equipment, this time flying in different areas. Again they were reported as successful.

BATTLE CLIMB AND WG CDR GILLAN'S RECORD

On 10 February 1938 a certain Wg Cdr Gillan was reported as having flown a Hawker Hurricane from Edinburgh to Northolt in the incredibly short time of forty minutes, giving a speed of 495 mph. This was the world's fastest aeroplane speed, but it could not be accepted as a record because it was flown one way only – the reverse direction would have to be flown in a given period of time, and the average of the two speeds taken to make an official record. This flight was in fact a freak trip! At 14.15 hours the same day we did a battle climb, taking off into a wind blowing from the north. We climbed on this northerly heading up to 30,000 feet and then descended – still heading north. When we had come down to about 5,000 feet we were about five miles *south* of the aerodrome we had left earlier, and at no time had we been flying any other heading than north! The answer to this was that we had been flying into an especially strong headwind at height. The wind had been so strong that we had been blown backwards in relation to the ground. Both the CO and the station meteorological officer saw this happen. They said that we disappeared climbing north of the aerodrome and then when we were in the region of 20,000 feet they saw the whole formation drift backwards across the aerodrome and to the south. This was the reason for Gillan's 'successful' flight south from Edinburgh – he must have had a following wind of nearly 200 mph! We later came to know more of these high winds at great altitudes, which came to be known as 'jetstreams'. So through this discovery John Gillan earned the nickname 'Downwind Gillan'.

Munich

Spring 1938 saw me engaged to be married, and there was a quiet wedding the following August, in Holy Trinity Church, Darlington. After a short honeymoon at Skelmorlie, where it rained most of the time, Elsie and I moved into a married quarter at Catterick.

We had hardly been in married quarters for a month when we had the first of the scares which heralded World War II. It was one weekend, on a Sunday morning, I believe, when an NCO knocked at our door with the order for me to report to the hangar immediately. By the time I arrived at the hangar the doors were being opened and the Furies were being pushed out. Armourers were busy working on the aircraft's Vickers guns with an obvious sense of quiet seriousness – the squadron was being brought up to a state of preparedness for something!

We were not told exactly the reason for this 'panic', or 'flap', but we had a pretty good idea. Although there was no obvious immediate need for this alert, there is no doubt that it had a useful purpose to remind us what we were in the RAF for, and it had the effect of removing some cobwebs and dust from the mobilisation scheme of the squadron. By the middle of the afternoon we were left with many thoughts of what the future held. We had been given a warning – and a very important breathing space.

Following this wretched Munich affair our flying activities seemed to take on a more urgent and realistic nature. There were more interception exercises with other squadrons and much more attention to methods of attack and invasion.

Controlling for an interception

The method of controlling a defending fighter against an intruding aircraft at this time was rather a Heath Robinson affair, to say the least. There was a radio location system being installed generally, and in our area it existed and was called RDF (radio direction finding) of which we were forbidden to speak, for obvious reasons, but it was a crude system compared to modern radar. It had a poor discrimination of the target and might give a stronger signal from a close flock of seabirds than it would from a single aircraft, especially if it was a wooden one. We often thought that reports of suspected aircraft were in fact sea birds, in whose bodies the oil added to the signal-reflecting qualities. These 'sightings' were characteristic in the way they used to 'pop up' and then disappear just as quickly as they appeared.

The accuracy of the plots was not good, especially with regard to height, and the signals the operator received needed considerable interpretation before they could be used effectively. Finally, the equipment could look only one way, and as the RDF stations were sited near the coast they could not plot overland and thus could not record the position of the outgoing fighters.

We had two-way radio, of course, but the standard of the aircraft set's performance was limited. The receiver required very careful and repeated tuning, and being in the HF band of frequencies the reception was subject to a fair amount of interference. As for navigation equipment, the aircraft carried nothing at all apart from the usual air-speed indicator, altimeter, turn-and-bank indicator and a magnetic compass. Each pilot was given a stopwatch to be held on his personal charge since it was an 'attractive item'. This watch was usually hung round the neck on a length of string since the watch holder fitted in the aircraft was intended for an ordinary watch, and was too far away in a remote part of the part of the cockpit where it could not be operated readily.

On the ground we had established an operations room where a navigation plotter could receive and plot on a table map the information received from the RDF stations, which was always considerably behind, of course, and whatever other information about the fighter position and height was available either from the fighter himself or from the local DF station. The plotter's calculation was in the main a dead-reckoning plot of the fighter from take-off using the courses, speeds and heights as ordered by the controller and using also the wind speeds and directions at the various heights as given by the meteorological officer, all in all a complicated job!

The accuracy of this plotting and thereafter the success of the interception depended largely on how accurately the pilot was able to fly to the instructions given by the controller, and in giving these instructions the controller had to be ever mindful of the fact that his plotted information was late and not very accurate, so that the only thing he could be sure about was that neither the target nor the fighter was in the position plotted, and that while the fighter was doing what he wanted it to do the target might have turned onto a new heading – or gone home! So wishful thinking and considerable anticipation seasoned with a large measure of good luck was essential.

The method of using the stopwatch in the navigation of the fighter was as follows. The fighter having been ordered off with a heading and height at which to fly flew round the aerodrome to set course, crossing the aerodrome at, say, 500 feet. As the pilot crossed the centre of the field he gave the controller and navigation plotter a 'zero', at the same time starting his stopwatch. From then on all flying had to be done on the instructions of the controller and at agreed suitable speeds, of course, there would be one speed for climbing and one for level flying and another for descending. An example of the controller's instruction would be, 'At Zero plus 3½ orbit (circle)'; then, 'At Zero plus 5 vector 090 angels fifteen'; and 'At Zero plus 7 Vector 110.' The occupation of the pilot, perhaps flying in cloud, can well be imagined, checking his stopwatch and watching the seconds tick by, waiting to start a new climb or turn onto a new heading at Zero plus 8½ – maintaining speed, height and direction, watching engine instruments, setting a new heading on the compass and operating the radio!

Then when the interception was over there was the job of getting back home, which if the controller was occupied with another interception was largely of the self-service kind, although one would usually get a course to steer and the approximate distance to go. These circumstances again did much to help me develop the capability of maintaining a mental plot of the whole flight so as to have a pretty good idea of my position at any time – mental DR.

Notes

1. 41 Squadron Motto: *Seek and destroy*. Badge: A double-armed cross. The badge is adapted from the Arms of Saint Omer, which was the squadron's first overseas headquarters and with which the squadron has since maintained a link.
2. Money flares – comprising a steel cage enclosing an asbestos wick soaked in paraffin, which burnt at the rate of 1¼ gallons an hour.

Effective through mist or low cloud, or at night. Three were laid at the upwind boundary of an ELG in an 'L' shape with the vertical leg pointing downwind, indicating the landing direction. Initially carried out by civilian volunteers, by the end of 1916 this was carried out by Royal Defence Corps detachments allocated to each site. Both squadron and flight landing grounds used flares to mark runways at night. [Paul Doyle's *Fields of the First*, Forward Airfield Research Publishing]

3. A canvas hood that could be moved to cover the cockpit so that the pilot could not see outside.
4. An early type of ground-based flight simulator.

CHAPTER 5

Spitfires!

We had known for some time that we would be getting Supermarine Spitfires, but the date was put back time after time. One reason was said to be that a sub-contractor making the wings had 'boobed' on a measurement so that they would not fit the fuselages! No. 19 Squadron at Duxford was to be first to get the new machines, and we were to be next on the list. I believe the CO of No. 19, Sqn Ldr J. Conyers, had got a Spitfire to take round the aerodromes to see if any airfields were unsuitable for the machine. He certainly came to Catterick and did a few landings.

Immediately after Christmas 1938 we began receiving the Spitfires. There was not a dual-controlled machine, so we were given some typewritten notes to read, and fuel and hydraulic systems diagrams to study. Then there was a lecture from our squadron CI, 'Fanny' Adams, on the handling of the Spitfire and especially pointing out the differences between the biplane and the monoplane. These notes were from HQ Fighter Command, I think. The handling of the Spitfire, we all appreciated, would be very different from that of the Fury, but with hindsight there is no doubt that the differences and the cautionary advice were overdone. For instance the quarter beam and other deflection types of attack were said to be impossible, and all attacks were to be made from the rear without deflection: this turned out not to be so. Also, in the event of engine failure we were advised not to attempt to carry out the recognised type of forced landing into wind, and such emergencies were to be handled with a forced landing straight ahead, irrespective of the direction of the wind – no 'S' turns to gain a favourable field or direction was advised.

Again experience showed that the old techniques still applied in perhaps some modified way.

My first trip in a Spitfire[1] was on 12 January 1939 after several periods of sitting in the cockpit getting to know the layout of controls and instruments. With a machine supported on trestles we operated the undercarriage, which had to be pumped up and down by hand. The propeller was a two-bladed, fixed-pitch, wooden one which wasn't very efficient, since the blade setting was designed for normal flying at a medium altitude. It was like trying to drive a car always in a middle gear – difficult to get going and slow to accelerate, and the engine running far too fast when travelling fast. During take-off the torque (the tendency for the engine to turn the aircraft in the opposite direction to the propeller) was quite marked, and one had to use all the throttle and power one could to get off uphill and on grass!

The first flight was a mixture of wonderment, exhilaration of course, and some trepidation, and it was a little awesome. The view from the cockpit was very restricted, absolutely blind in front and for about thirty degrees either side. The excessive torque with full throttle which was necessary could be felt pressing the port wheel into the turf and the plane trying to turn over. The first hundred yards or so were a rather slow lumbering acceleration, and one began to wonder whether one would get off the ground, but as the speed built up and the tail rose the machine hauled itself into the air. Then the speed increased rapidly and the altimeter began winding up at a rate never seen before. After a brief spell of near amazement I remembered that the under-carriage had to be got up. A change of hands on the stick, select up and pump with the right hand. From the ground a first solo is usually noticeable by the aircraft bobbing up and down as the undercarriage is pumped up after take-off, for in pulling and pushing the pump handle with the right hand one tends to move the left hand – so up, down, up, down! Anyway I found myself doing this. With two red lights showing that the undercarriage was unlocked the pumping continued until the indicator lamps showed the wheels were up.

In what seemed to be less that a minute I was about five miles from the aerodrome and at 4,000 feet. It seemed almost unreal in a sense. Then after a few turns and a wide circuit of the aerodrome came the approach and landing. A look at the airspeed indicator showed that the speed was too high to put the undercarriage down. Throttling back the engine almost scared me out of my wits – the klaxon horn came on and shrieked in my ears to warn me that the undercarriage was not down! Opening the throttle slightly got rid of that awful noise, and eventually the speed dropped enough to put the wheels down – select down and pump again – two red lights and two greens – safely locked down. Downwind and a gentle turn to the left across wind, flaps down and the final turn in, trimming back slightly as the speed dropped off. Once again that huge long and broad nose blotted out the view directly ahead. Keeping the engine pulling gently the aircraft seemed almost to land itself, and I could hardly feel the touchdown. A great experience and quite a step from the Fury and the Demon.

We continued our operational training on the Spitfires, and after some twenty hours by day we flew them at night. By the end of June the whole squadron had achieved the conversion, twenty hours by day and five by night. All this on a restricted grass aerodrome and with the wooden propellers.

Only one pilot, a reservist sergeant, had difficulty on his first solo. He bent the aeroplane on landing, not very badly, and as was the custom then he was given advice and another aeroplane – the second try was not a very good effort, either, but better than the first. Perhaps this was a bad omen, for this pilot was killed later. There was no obvious reason for his crash but a post mortem showed a high carbon dioxide (CO_2) content in his blood. There was a suggestion that this chap had absorbed the CO_2 from a coke-burning combustion stove in a hut.

THE LAST EMPIRE AIR DAY DISPLAY

On 19 May 1939, together with several other squadrons, we took part in a mass formation of sixty-three aircraft. The main route was to Digby, Grantham, Nottingham, Rotherham, Sheffield and back to Catterick. I suspect this flight was intended to be a morale booster for the public by showing it that we had 'squadrons' of Spitfires and Hurricanes. Then on the 20th we gave our last Empire Air Display at Catterick, which was largely confined to formation air drill.

PROMOTION

My 'crown' came through on 1 June and saw me promoted to flight sergeant.

PIP SQUEAK

We continued our operational training with more and more affiliation and interception exercises, and although we still had the old TR9 radio we did get a new and valuable aid to assist the plotting of our positions. This was called 'Pip Squeak', no doubt because that was the noise it made on the radio. It was a simple device really and was fitted to every aircraft. It consisted of an electrically operated clockwork switch with a pointer on the clock face completing one revolution in one minute, just like the second hand of a watch. A red-painted quadrant was painted on the clock face between 12 o'clock and 3 o'clock, and the pointer was arranged to switch on the radio transmitter when moving through the red quadrant. The harmonic signal transmitted was picked up and triangulated by the direction-finding (DF) stations to fix the position of the aircraft.

There were two switches for the pilot to operate: one was an ON-OFF switch to set the clock going, and this was usually set to a Zero given by the ground controller to coincide with his clock and therefore to identify a particular aircraft. The other switch was an IN-OUT switch which controlled Pip Squeak's connection to the radio transmitter, thus enabling the pilot to allow the signal to be transmitted only when required, and yet to keep the clock working in time with the original setting.

It was usual for all the aircraft in the squadron four formations to have their Pip Squeaks 'on' and synchronised, but only one would respond to the controller's instruction to 'pip in' and 'pip out'. However, by synchronising four different formations to the four different quarters of the Pip Squeak's dial, for example Red Section 12-3, Blue 3-6, Yellow 6-9 and Green 9-12, it was possible if all four formations were told to 'pip in', the controller could get a fix on each, every minute continuously. Pip Squeak was a very welcome addition to our equipment, and on the whole it worked very well. Occasionally the clock might stop for no apparent reason, but another trouble was that in bumpy weather the clocks would often miss a beat and you might want only fourteen of these bumps to put out the synchronisation completely: each quarter-section of the dial was of fourteen seconds, thus leaving a gap of one second between sectors or quadrants.

PRACTICE INTERCEPTIONS ON THE GROUND

Writing this in December 1973 after seeing that a course of pilots passing out at Linton-on-Ouse did their traditional flypast on cycles because of the current fuel crisis reminded me of the following unexpected event. One day when our battle flight, which was 'A' Flight, was airborne on the battle climb, orders came through from Group HQ at Hucknall that the flight was to land at Hucknall. They were met by 'Daddy' Probyn. He told them to keep their helmets on and to their amazement gave each a butcher boy's type of cycle with a TR9 radio set in the carrier! They then had to ride the cycles in formation to the orders of a controller over the radio from the control tower. They were to intercept an 'enemy' formation approaching them, and – a further surprise – out from between two hangars came an 'enemy' formation of 'cycle planes'. The interception and attack completed to the satisfaction of a smiling, twinkling-eyed 'Daddy' Probyn, they flew back to Catterick for a rather late lunch.

FLYING ACCIDENT

On 18 July 1939 Sgt Plt Kenneth Mitchell was killed when he flew into Great Dun Fell in the Pennines in Supermarine Spitfire I, K9888. Mitchell had taken off from Catterick on a cross-country exercise to RAF Kingstown, near Carlisle, which necessitated him crossing the mountain range separating the two bases. Part-way through the flight, but apparently after Mitchell had already crossed the mountains, the exercise was called off due to the deteriorating weather. Accordingly, Mitchell turned back for Catterick, but as he approached the range on his southward journey, visibility dropped to almost nothing. Attempting to re-cross the Pennines in these conditions, Mitchell flew into Great Dun Fell at an altitude of 2,500 feet, about five miles north-east of

Knock village, by Appleby in Cumbria. The aircraft exploded on impact, killing Mitchell instantly. The crash site was found the following day by a local shepherd near the peak. Blame for the accident was officially placed on the Station Commander for having allowed the exercise to commence in the first place.[2]

The summer months of 1939 were an unsettling time for us. We knew that war was inevitable, but when? How long had we got? We still awaited the variable-pitch airscrews for the Spitfires which would mean so much more in performance. The Tannoy public address system that would broadcast air raid warnings and operational messages had yet to be installed. Reserve pilots were coming in and the local auxiliary No. 609 Squadron was needing help in becoming operational, not only in the flying of the Spitfire but in tactics and interception procedures. There was a lot to do and perhaps not much time in which to do it. At last the Rolls-Royce engineers arrived, and soon we had fitted the two-speed, metal, three-bladed airscrews, instead of the fixed-pitch, wooden two-bladers. These would give us a fine-pitch position for take-off and a coarse pitch for all other flying – a great improvement for a quicker and safer take-off, and when in 'top gear' much less chance of damaging the engine by over-revving it.

We lost one pilot about this time through inexperience and the inevitable 'finger trouble' which affected most of us at one time or another. This young chap was doing circuits and landings in a Spitfire and had quite successfully done several when he took off again, possibly in coarse pitch but certainly with his flaps down. Inevitably his take-off was very slow and laboured, and the initial climb much reduced, with the result that he struck the top of the control tower with his undercarriage and crashed behind it near one of the hangars. We saw him at close quarters taxi back for this last take-off, and he had his flaps up, which was correct – so he must have put them down when he did his pre-take-off check. I may point out that the flaps of the Spitfire had no intermediate position for take-off and that in operation they were either up or down.

'CRACK EM' STATON

Our affiliation exercises brought us into contact at Dishforth with the CO of No. 9 Bomber Squadron, Wg Cdr W.E. Staton, known as 'Big Bill', or 'Crack-em' Staton. He was big and tough with a square jaw and had a terrific morale. His squadron was flying Whitleys and he declared that no fighter would ever get him! The outbreak of war saw him leading 'Gumphlet', or leaflet, raids on Germany, and then the first bombing of Sylt in which he flew up and down at quite low altitude to draw the anti-aircraft fire from the other aircraft so that they could concentrate on bombing accurately! His leadership was so good and confident that his squadron had remarkably fewer casualties than did his fellow squadron, No. 10 at Dishforth. 'Big Bill' Staton took the part of the station commander in the well-known war film 'F for Freddie'. He was a crack shot but ended the war in a Japanese POW camp as an air commodore, where he no doubt made his mark morale-wise too.

THE GRAF ZEPPELIN

On 3 August 1939 we were alerted with the news that the Graf Zeppelin was flying up the east coast, but as it was well out of territorial waters we were not allowed to intercept, much to the disappointment of us all. This was the second known, and plotted, flight of the airship along the coast with the obvious intention of monitoring the signals from our early-type radar stations. Both flights were said to be abortive. Two fighters were sent off from Dyce, and these positively identified the airship on this second flight.

FIFTH COLUMN

For some weeks during the late summer of 1939 the civilian contractors had been painting up the camp, and a couple of painters were at work on our hangar, which housed a row of offices along the front wall and facing the aerodrome. One of our more elderly corporals, a rigger who had served in World War I and who had been a POW, came into the office one day and suggested with a certain degree of feeling that the man who was painting the outside of our office window had been working on that window for far too long and had spent much more time watching the activities on the tarmac with the aircraft than in doing his painting. He suggested that the man was a fifth columnist! At first the Flight Sergeant, 'Dusty' Coleman, wouldn't listen, but when the corporal insisted, 'Dusty' gave in and went off to see the Station Warrant Officer. He came back a few minutes later with the SWO and the NCO in charge of the RAF Police. The painter was approached and after some conversation went away with the policeman. He never returned, and much to our corporal's satisfaction we were informed that the painter was indeed a fifth columnist. His lodgings in the village had been searched and provided the necessary evidence.

A SPY?

In setting up our operations room we needed controllers. In the early stages the pilots in the squadron had taken turns to work in the operations room, but soon we had reservists posted in for the job. One of them was a flight lieutenant ex-pilot of WWI who became what we assumed to be our senior controller. He certainly was efficient and we liked flying under his control. However, the day before war was declared he disappeared from the camp and was never seen again at Catterick. Rumour had it that a German submarine picked him up off the coast near Hartlepool!

WAR DECLARED

Our last operational flying before the declaration of war was a three-day air defence exercise based at Digby, and on return to Catterick I occupied myself for a couple of days giving instrument flying in the Magister to four new pilots. Then came the final preparations, training ceased and all serviceable aircraft were armed up, radio frequencies changed, as were the call signs, oxygen was checked and the aircraft dispersed to the more remote corners of the aerodrome on the eastern side next to the River Swale. This would give us a quick take-off to the north-west or south-west, which would be the longest two runs as near as possible into the prevailing wind direction.

Tents were put up at the dispersal points with a field telephone to each flight from the operations room, and armed guards were introduced. Slit trenches were dug and latrines with a few 'thunder-boxes' were installed.

It was certain that everything we were doing was in preparation for war, but at the same time no one seemed to voice the opinion or show that war was near or inevitable. Perhaps there would be a last-minute solution, and Winston Churchill's gathering storm would in some miraculous way blow over. It was obvious that in any case we must do all we could to be prepared, and that was what was happening around us.

On that morning of 3 September the usual Sunday joint of beef was roasting in the oven and Elsie was preparing the vegetables. The day did not seem to be an extraordinarily important one to us and we were following a usual quiet Sunday routine. No doubt because the previous scares and periods of tension had seemed to come to nothing, we had become complacent – but the relative, if rather uneasy, calm of the day was shattered at eleven o'clock by that memorable radio broadcast by the prime minister Neville Chamberlain that 'we are now at war with Germany'.

It is difficult to describe our feelings on hearing this momentous news. Although we were somehow prepared for it, perhaps we had clung too much on the chance that it wouldn't happen, but the announcement shocked us deeply and we felt quite depressed among other things. Our thoughts naturally turned to ourselves having been married just a year – what would become of us? And where would it all end? The rest of the day took on a sombre tone. The immediate change was in radio programmes, with music to suit the occasion and the news bulletins, to which we listened religiously. There was nothing to lighten the gloomy outlook; on the contrary a report that the air raid sirens in London had sounded did not help, in spite of the warning being a false alarm. There was definitely an air of despair at No. 32 Airmen's Married Quarter (AMQ) which no doubt was shared by many. While living in the married quarters we invited Dorethea Jeff to stay with us. Dorethea was Elsie's half-sister.

Our minds were in a bit of a whirl, and fearing the worst, it was difficult to think sensibly and decide what to do for the best. Should we pack up our married quarter and Elsie go home to Darlington? As I knew that there was no plan for the squadron to move, we decided to sit tight and stay put. There was always the chance of the aerodrome being attacked, but Darlington, an important industrial town on the main-line railway between London and the north, was perhaps an equally likely target.

So it was war at last, after the scares, the appeasements, the hopes and the fears. After the long-drawn-out and unsettling days of 1938 and 1939 the future was at last known – and yet unknown! We at least knew which way we were heading, but what to, when and where, and how would we fare? I had done about seventy-eight flying hours on the Spitfire, but one never felt ready for real action.

No. 26 Squadron, our neighbouring squadron, now equipped with Westland Lysanders, went to France with the Advanced Air Striking Force, and a new squadron of night-fighters, No. 219, was formed and took residence, but without the Bristol Blenheims which they were to get.

Our squadron was brought up to war 'readiness' from first light on Monday 4 September. For several days no aircraft left the ground, and obviously this could not continue, so the flight that was not at readiness was allowed to carry on with selected flying. Later still, the section that was 'available ten minutes' was permitted to do occasional limited flying. Because all aircraft were fully armed those airborne could be used even more quickly than the 'readiness' section on the ground. However, all flying was done strictly under the authority and control of the operations room, for obvious reasons, and no one was allowed to cross the coast nor go near the gun-defended areas without their controllers' permission; then there were barrage balloons to avoid at Middlesbrough and Newcastle.

During the remainder of September I did only four hours' flying, mostly aircraft tests, formation and practice attacks. The latter were with No. 609 Squadron (Flg Off Edge) against No. 9 Squadron with Whitleys (Wg Cdr Staton) at Dishforth. The remainder of our time was spent either waiting in flying kit at dispersal working on our aircraft or improving the facilities for the anticipated action to come. There was also plenty of intelligence reading to do and trying to absorb the many operational and security instructions that were issued daily. One of these which were changed daily was the 'colour' and 'letter' of the day. These were codes to be fired by Very light or flashed by identification lamp if challenged or fired on by a friendly aircraft or the anti-aircraft (AA) guns. Then there was the 'password' of the day for moving about the camp – the recently acquired armed guards of Army reservists were dead keen to challenge anyone by day or night, so it paid us all to have the correct password on the tip of the tongue!

NOTES

1. Spitfire Mk I K9835.
2. Steve Brew.

CHAPTER 6

Preparing for Action

Our squadron was brought up to war 'readiness' from first light on Monday 4 September 1939. This meant that one section of three aircraft was to be kept ready to be airborne within five minutes, and a second section to be available to be airborne within ten minutes. The other aircraft were permitted to remain at various states of availability extending to being released from operations entirely. This routine was maintained throughout the hours of daylight, and at night the flights took it in turns to have one section sleeping, but clothed, at dispersal and the other section also sleeping at dispersal but sleeping in a more relaxed fashion. The flare-path was laid out but not lit. The aircraft, if ordered off at night, would operate singly and, the airfield runway 'flares' being hooded, electric 'glim' lamps would be lit quickly enough.

Two sections of three pilots would be at readiness when the telephone from the operations room would ring: 'Scramble, Blue Section'. Before the telephone could be replaced three pilots already wearing Mae Wests would charge through the bell tent flap running like hares to their aircraft. Ground crew would be doing the same. Leaping onto the wing and into the cockpit seat, the pilot would find the rigger on the other wing ready to assist with fastening harnesses. The pilot would then switch on petrol cocks, prime the engine if required, put on his helmet, plug in and switch on the radio and call for the instructions regarding height and vector,[1] check the airscrew pitch, check the trimming tabs, lock harness, switch magneto on and signal to ground crew to start the Merlin using the battery trolley unit. As the engine fired the pilot would signal to the ground crew to remove the wheel chocks and the leader would open the throttles and surge forward with a weaving movement due to reduced forward visibility.

The engines of the aircraft kept at readiness were always kept warm, so without delay the three aircraft could leave the sandbagged dispersal area and accelerate straight across the grass airfield into wind. As soon as the aircraft had left the ground the undercarriage would be retracted to increase speed. The Number 2 and Number 3 aircraft would close up tight to the leader of the flight, and the three Spitfires would bank over steeply in a tight turn to the correct heading and climb steeply and disappear in a few moments, leaving the airfield quiet once again.

We thought about the future and how any encounters with enemy aircraft would be handled mentally. We knew about the dangers. Flying in tight formation there was always the risk of collision with a wing-man, and during the interception collision with an enemy aircraft was another risk, although at the time I think we did not know how big a risk this was. The armour plating on the Spitfire was minimal, and this was known to stop bullets when fired at over 200 yards. Under 200 yards the bullets would penetrate. We had de Wilde incendiary shells and we suspected that the Germans had something similar. We imagined that incendiary or explosive cannon shells would make a mess of a pilot if he was hit. We thought about the possibility of bullets striking oxygen bottles or petrol tanks and the resultant explosion or inferno. Fire was the first and the worst fear. We sat behind 85 gallons of high-octane petrol, and the thought of this igniting made one sweat. We had parachutes, of course, but no opportunity to practise bale-outs, so all the pilots had their pet methods which they mentally rehearsed over and over again. Forced landings on terra firma we imagined would be similar to any other situation in another aircraft with an engine failure.

Forced landings, or 'ditching', on water were a different matter, and at this time no one had a clue how the Spitfire would behave or how long one had to get out. The Spitfire had a heavy front end with the weight of the engine. We knew that the low water temperature of the North Sea or the English Channel was the final enemy of those unlucky enough to 'ditch' or to parachute into the sea. We mentally rehearsed the procedure for getting out of the wet, heavy parachute harness and then the job of blowing up the life-jacket through the rubber tube. It was easy on the ground! What would it be like if the sea was rough or if one was injured? What was the chance of survival in the cold water? Would one be picked up? After a while we stopped worrying. Some hoped for a bullet rather than the slow or painful death of water or fire.

We were very much aware of the need to learn quickly the tactics and 'tricks' of survival in combat. We knew luck would play a big part in survival. Some of us had training on interception and attack procedure but we did not know how we would fare when tested for real.

The official theory before the war was that England would be attacked by long-range bombers without fighter escorts, as the fighters had limited range due to small fuel capacity. We were told that the bombers would be in tight, massed formations and interceptions would be carried out according to six basic patterns. These were described in the training manual. We rehearsed these drills.

In Fighter Attack 1 a section of fighters would move into line astern and each aircraft would attack the lone bomber directly from behind, break away and then let the second fighter fire a burst, and so on. In Fighter Attack 2 the intercepting fighters would attack from below in a climbing attitude and in line astern. Fighter Attack 3 involved the whole section flying in vic formation and firing together on a group of bombers. Fighter Attack 4 used the vic formation to attack a group of bombers from below. Fighter Attack 5 used a line-abreast formation to attack a group of bombers. Fighter Attack 6 was a complex procedure involving the whole squadron. To employ the appropriate attack procedure required judgement, communication and then discipline. The targets would not be expected to sit still, and some degree of improvisation was deemed as being necessary.

As it turned out, the bombers were often escorted when they came in tight formations to concentrate both their bombing patterns and their defensive firepower. Occasionally a lone bomber might be encountered.

Squadron organisation

Fighter squadrons generally consisted of twelve aircraft, with a reserve of pilots and aircraft maintained to allow for servicing and personnel absence through sickness, leave or training. These twelve aircraft were divided into two flights, 'A' and 'B'. Each flight would be the responsibility of a flight commander, usually of flight lieutenant rank or above.

Operationally, the squadron would be led by the squadron leader, taking the role of one of the flight commanders, or by the most senior – or in some cases, most experienced – flight commander. Each flight was divided into two sections, or vics of three aircraft. 'A' Flight was divided into Red and Yellow sections, with 'B' Flight consisting of Blue and Green sections. The aircraft within the sections were known as 1, 2 and 3 respectively. Each section was appointed a section leader, again determined by rank or experience.

When airborne, the location of the section within the flight, or indeed squadron, was not important. Thus, Green 1 of 'B' Flight might be the squadron leader, who was, in turn, also the flight commander and the section leader. The identification of each aircraft by this designation made the responsibilities of each pilot clear, and was an effective method for radio communication and squadron administration.

Search and cruise formations consisted of each flight either echeloned to both sides, or both echeloned to one side – port or starboard. This rigid formation made manoeuvring difficult, and relied heavily on each pilot controlling his throttle to maintain position in the formation. In some instances, a single aircraft would be used at the rear of the formation, generally at a greater height, theoretically to provide early warning of attack.

Luftwaffe bombers often flew in a small group of three called a *Kette*. This was similar to the RAF vic. *Luftwaffe* fighters flew in widely spaced groups of four called a *Schwarm*. Each *Schwarm* consisted of two pairs, or *Rotten*. The leading aircraft in the *Rotten* took on the offensive role, and the second of the pair had the job of protecting the leader. Two pairs of *Rotten* made up a *Schwarm*. A *Staffel* consisted of three *Schwarms*. The pairs would be staggered in both position and height. The formation was defensive, flexible, aggressive and simple for the pilots to follow. It also afforded all pilots good visibility for spotting distant aircraft. In the event of an interception the two pairs could split up and protect each other in a sandwich manoeuvre.[2]

FIGHTER COMMAND STRUCTURE

The British Isles were divided into four groups, numbered sequentially from south-west England to Scotland: 10, 11, 12 and 13. The airspace in each group was divided into sectors, with all activity within the boundaries of that sector being controlled from a single sector station. This sector station might be an airfield or separate RAF station, with each sector allocated a single letter identity.

The major airfields within each sector maintained a minimum operational strength of three fighter squadrons. For example, 41, 222 and 603 Fighter Squadrons were stationed at Hornchurch in early September 1940. However, squadrons or elements of squadrons were often dispersed to the various adjacent, smaller satellite airfields – such as Rochford – when full-scale attacks on airfields became a *Luftwaffe* priority.

When airborne, each squadron was controlled by the operations room at the relevant sector station. A series of coded call-signs[3] were adopted to make communications shorter and, hopefully, to confuse enemy forces monitoring radio traffic.

The tote board at each operations room listed each squadron above an electrically lit listings board which gave the controller immediate knowledge of the operational status of all squadrons within his sector. Squadrons could be at READINESS – meaning pilots at their dispersal areas with flying equipment worn or at hand; STANDBY – with pilots sitting in aircraft fully prepared for take-off; or they could be called to SCRAMBLE – immediate take-off, generally within three minutes of the order. Pilots and aircrew might be required to be available, meaning within earshot of the Tannoy system or station telephone.

NO. 41 SQUADRON

During the 'hard lying', or 'roughing it', in the tents, the Squadron Ground Crew Flight Sergeant managed to persuade the Station Equipment Officer that King's Regulations permitted the issue of rum under these conditions. This was doled out until one ground-crew airman passed out. A surplus supply of rum found its way into the tent occupied by 'Wally' Wallens and 'Cowboy' Blatchford. One night 'Cowboy' and 'Wally' were at readiness, and as the weather was hot and humid they were both sensibly attired in their pyjamas. Their theory was that if there was a scramble they could get dressed very quickly, put on their Mae Wests and no one would be the wiser. The effect of a couple of tots of rum seemed to increase the temperature, and 'Cowboy' removed his pyjama jacket. The operations room phone rang and called for a single aircraft scramble. Normally such calls might be for a twenty-minute sortie at about 5,000 feet before the aircraft was recalled to land, or 'pancake',[4] as it was called. 'Cowboy' ran to his Spitfire in pyjama bottoms and a Mae West, leaving 'Wally' in charge of the unfinished rum. The Spitfire cockpit is pretty warm up to a few thousand feet, at which point it becomes progressively cooler until it falls well below zero. 'Cowboy' was unlucky, as Control sent him to 15,000 feet, and he had to patrol up there for over an hour. When he finally returned he was a shaking, shivering, half-naked frozen figure, and had to be helped out of the cockpit and back to the tent for a defrosting in front of the red-hot stove. 'Cowboy' had radioed 'Bully', the controller, after half an hour into his patrol to explain his predicament. Apparently all 'Bully' said was, 'Stay where you are; we will bring you a nice cup of Ovaltine and tuck you in.' 'Bully' then started singing, 'We are the Ovaltineys, little girls and boys ...'[5]

'OUTBREAK OF WAR' ON 1 OCTOBER 1939

October 1939 came with no sign of the war beginning in our area. In the first two weeks I flew two hours simulating air attacks on our ground defences, and on 16 October I went back to the Magister to give one of our sergeant pilots some more instrument flying. That same day we heard that a number of German bombers had raided the Forth area and that these had been intercepted by a Scottish auxiliary squadron with three confirmed kills – these being the first of the war at home. We had neither seen nor heard of any activity except for one or two false alarms that turned out to be our own coastal Avro Ansons which got us no further than getting into our cockpits. I believe at this time there was a case of an Anson being attacked by one of our own aircraft, and we were warned to be very careful and to be absolutely sure that any target of ours was in fact hostile.

Our position at Catterick was ideal to protect the industrial area in and around the Tees valley, including Middlesbrough, Stockton and Darlington. Teesside was heavily defended with heavy and light artillery, and over forty-five barrage balloons. There were three radar stations at Danby Beacon, Goldthorpe and Shotton. There were also ten observation posts manned by the Royal Observer Corps. Middlesbrough was a centre for engineering and armament manufacture. Notable companies were the Acklam Britannia Steel Works, Gjers, Mills, Dorman and Long, Furness Shipyard and the ICI chemical plant.

Notes

1. Course to steer. German equivalent was Caruso.
2. Information provided by Stephen Bungay.
3. Examples of these call-signs, and those used by the *Luftwaffe*, are listed within a website: http://brew.clients.ch/RAF41Sqdn.htm
4. Land, refuel and rearm.
5. Story told by 'Wally' Wallens.

CHAPTER 7

Action at Last!

Green Section encounters a Heinkel

On 17 October 1939, in the afternoon, my own Green Section was at readiness, Flg Off 'Cowboy' Blatchford (a Canadian) was the leader, I was Number Two and Sgt Albert 'Bill' Harris Number Three. We were rather bored with our lot of forever waiting, and we were relaxing in our tent shortly before four o'clock in the afternoon when we were jerked to our feet by the ringing of the field telephone. Perhaps it was another false alarm or just another administrative message. 'Cowboy' picked up the receiver – 'an unidentified aircraft off Whitby flying up the coast' – we were off at last. The short 'Green Section Scramble' echoed through the dispersal as the crews raced to the machines. Our parachutes were already in the aircraft and we rushed to them, putting on our helmets and oxygen masks. Each member of the ground crew knew just what to do to help the pilot to strap in and start up. At five minutes to four we were airborne. I was flying Spitfire K9805,[1] and after taking off we climbed to 9,000 feet in the direction of West Hartlepool. As we approached Middlesbrough, 'Cowboy' turned south to fly down the coast on the landward side so that we were looking down the sun out to sea. The visibility was rather hazy and we were flying in open vic, which was the usual formation when searching. My position on the leader's left gave me the best opportunity and responsibility to search towards the sea.

We had just passed Saltburn when I spotted an aircraft flying north some distance out to sea, but I could not identify it. I immediately reported its position relative to us, to 'Cowboy', by

RT using the accepted 'clock-code', in this case 'ten o'clock level'. In spite of a couple of attempts to point out the aircraft in this fashion, 'Cowboy' could not see it, nor could Albert 'Bill' Harris. Finally I adopted a procedure, not official, but one that we had agreed upon, which was to lead the section towards the target. I broke away and said, 'Follow me'. 'Cowboy' and Harris followed me. After turning and then making a direct heading towards the aircraft I was still the only one who could see the target. Neither of my companions could see it due to the haze. 'Cowboy' and Albert 'Bill' Harris followed me in line astern.

I imagined that it might be another Anson, but the moment we had turned I saw it turn sharply seaward. This made me suspicious, especially as it seemed to be diving slightly as if trying to get away. On my opening up the Merlin engine to the 'gate'[2] the Spitfire surged forward and I quickly began to catch up. We had been severely warned about making sure of the identity of all target aircraft before we attacked.

I was determined to see the black crosses before shooting. So I dived below the aircraft, keeping directly behind and below, keeping out of the possible line of fire of the upper turret gun. Getting well below, nearly a thousand feet and slightly behind, I saw very clearly those black crosses against the pale blue of the undersides of the wings – it was a Heinkel 111K. I reported the identity by RT and I am sure I felt really sorry that it was an enemy plane. Then, pulling myself together, I realised what I was there to do and I pulled up to a position about five hundred yards behind. Closing into about four hundred and fifty yards with my gunsight switches on and set, I turned the safety catch of the gun firing button to 'fire' and pressed the button. The Spitfire's eight .303 Browning machine-guns unleashed a stream of hot metal. The answer I got back was a stream of tracer bullets from the upper turret gun, but fortunately these seemed to pass harmlessly by on my port side. Still closing in slightly I fired again, using up all my ammunition in fifteen seconds – just over 2,000 rounds. The upper gunner ceased firing and both the engines of the Heinkel started smoking. At this moment the Spitfire was buffeted by turbulence as I flew into the slipstream of the Heinkel. I realised that I was getting too close. As the Heinkel was now obviously descending to ditch into the sea I broke away to starboard. 'Cowboy' and Harris were no doubt somewhere behind me, although I could not see them. They continued with the attack. 'Cowboy' was keen, and in his haste to catch up with the Heinkel he approached too fast and overshot and nearly collided with the tailplane. All his ammunition was used in one burst. The dorsal gun on the Heinkel was silent. The Heinkel was losing height quite rapidly now, and as I was flying round I felt that both my legs were wet and I saw that there were beads of liquid all over the dashboard and instruments. My first thought was that I might have been hit and that either the petrol or the glycol coolant was leaking – more likely the latter as there was no obvious smell of petrol. As I was some twenty miles out to sea, not very high and believe it or not – to my shame – I had stupidly forgotten to put on my 'Mae West' life-jacket, I decided it would be prudent to return back to base independently and without delay.

Well, I was not hit and I got back safely, and after some thought I found that my wet legs and cockpit were due to rain-water that had collected in the bottom of the fuselage over the past weeks and had been thrown up into the cockpit when I hit the slip-stream of the Heinkel. The Spitfire was completely untouched! Almost before I had switched off my engine the CO of the newly formed 219 Squadron was leaning over the cockpit wanting to know all about this first combat and success – he was Sqn Ldr R.L.R. Acherley – 'Batchy'. 'Cowboy' and Harris followed me back and landed soon afterwards. Together we made out our combat reports and answered the eager and almost innumerable questions from the Station Commander down to the local tea boy.

'Cowboy' had watched the Heinkel ditch in the sea and saw two crew get into a rubber dinghy before the aircraft sank. One of the crew seemed to be injured in the leg. 'Cowboy' had circled the dinghy for a while and radioed the position of the airmen. He was told by our controller that a rescue boat was going out from Middlesbrough to pick up the survivors. We felt fairly satisfied with this, and as it wouldn't be dark for some hours we thought the pick-up would be successful. After tea and while we were still at dispersal a congratulatory signal came from the AOC of 13 Group at Ouston, near Newcastle. Then from the officers' mess came a bottle of champagne, which we emptied without much trouble.

This first sighting, encounter and shooting down of an enemy aircraft caused some very mixed feelings. First there was a feeling of regret that an enemy had been sighted at all, and then the immediate realisation of the inevitability of the situation. The attack had to be pressed home once identification at close quarters had been made or the risk of being shot down first was real enough. On the whole I cannot say I was elated.

My log-book entry reads very factually, as follows:

Date and hour	Aeroplane type and No.	Pilot	Time	Height	Course	Remarks
17/10/39 1555	Spitfire K9805	Self	1:00	9,000	Middlesboro' – Whitby	Operational patrol 1 Heinkel 111K shot down

Although I felt far from being elated, the spirits of the squadron and particularly those of our own flight received a boost by this event, and the increased keenness of everyone and especially of the ground crews was quite obvious. Although we were told that the German survivors were being picked up, for some reason this was found not to be true, for they came ashore at Sandsend some forty-eight hours later, and were taken to Middlesbrough hospital. I asked to go and see them and to take some cigarettes and chocolates for them, but I was refused this wish, which I thought to be quite reasonable. This made me feel even worse than I did when I found that we had been let down over the promised pick-up. A memento of that first combat was a 9 mm Luger pistol which was passed on to the squadron by the Military Police following the arrest of the German air crew. I saw it once in the squadron safe, and wonder now where it might be. The two survivors of the Heinkel became the first German fliers to be captured on English soil.

Much later, in 1979 in fact, more information came to light[3] regarding the above encounter. The Heinkel 111K involved in the above interception carried the markings F6 + PK and came from 2(F)/*Aufklarunggruppe* 122.[4] The crew comprised *Oberfeldwebel* Eugen Lange (pilot), *Unteroffiziers* Bernhard Hochstuhl (radio operator), Hugo Sauer (gunner) and *Leutnant* Joachim Kretschmer. Their mission was to locate the battle cruiser HMS *Hood*, which was believed to be in the Firth of Forth. The flight up the north-east coast was the second sortie of the day after their first was aborted near Edinburgh with no sign of HMS *Hood*.

Eugen Lange recalls the first sortie of the day:

> We reached the Firth of Forth at a height of about 6,000 metres. There was thick cloud cover at 2,000 metres. How could we get under the cloud without being seen to do a low-level flight to photograph the docks? Before we were decided on tactics ... we saw three black dots climbing out of the cloud ... There was no alternative, we made off to the east in the hope that the three fighters wouldn't be able to reach our height. After some time we bravely turned westwards again.

Bill Norman describes the events:

> Soon the Heinkel was travelling north again on their second approach, this time at 10,000 feet. At about 4.30 p.m. the three Spitfires from 41 Squadron (Shipman, Harris and Blatchford) attacked. Shipman attacked first. When 'Cowboy' Blatchford pressed home his attack from 400 yards there was no sign of Sauer, the gunner, as he had been shot through the body or his colleague Kretschmer had been shot through the head. Both had been killed instantly. Hochstuhl was lucky when a bullet grazed his flying helmet. Lange had been lucky too. His goggles were pierced by a bullet that then grazed his earphones. He was unmarked. The Heinkel was without any defence and with both engines damaged was in severe difficulties. Harris had the job of finishing off the Heinkel. The Heinkel glided low over the rough sea and finally smacked down in a cascade of spray twenty miles east of Whitby. The impact stopped Lange's watch at 5.00 p.m. With the departure of the two Spitfires (Harris and Blatchford) the German pilots faced a bleak prospect. Time was not on their side. Hochstuhl had taken the initiative and with a wounded leg had managed to release the rubber dinghy and inflate it. As soon as they climbed in the dinghy the plane sank with their survival rations. The two airmen spent a most uncomfortable, wet, cold and sleepless night. They paddled the dinghy with their bare hands to try and reach land. Several times they fired Very distress flares – all to no avail.

When darkness fell on the second night Lange was showing signs of exposure. More Very distress flares were fired – still no response.

Whitby and Runswick Bay lifeboats were in fact searching the North Sea following the sighting of the earlier flares, but the search proved useless. On the morning of 19 October the two airmen saw the Yorkshire cliffs. By this time they were too weak to paddle, but luck was on their side for a current carried the dinghy towards the shore and they landed on Lythedale Sands at the foot of a 150 ft cliff, just north of Sandsend village. LNER Special Constable George Thomas was at the top of the cliff guarding the entrance to a railway tunnel, and he found Hochstuhl gasping in broken English, 'I am a German flier, my friend is below and needs help ... where am I – near the Firth of Forth?' After a short struggle Hochstuhl was taken to Sandsend. George Thomas, Frank Dring and a policeman called Jack Barker found Lange close to death and still lying in the dinghy on the beach. The dinghy was deflated and used as a stretcher to carry Lange up the steep cliff-side path. The police took the men to Whitby, and as they departed Bernhard Hochstuhl gave George Thomas a packet of German cigarettes as a token of his gratitude. George Thomas said, 'They were quite decent fellows. One of them said, "I don't know what we are fighting for. I shall not smoke these cigarettes, but I may have one when there is somebody else in charge in Germany and peace is declared."'

On arrival at Whitby police station Lange was thawed out in a hot bath by Police Sergeant John Dunning. After a transfer to hospital Lange was found to be suffering from frostbite and exposure. Hochstuhl had sustained a shrapnel wound in one leg. Night Sister Winifred Wilson found that Hochstuhl was 'very charming and highly appreciative of all that was being done for them', while Lange was 'very stiff and highly suspicious'. Bernard Hochstuhl gave Winifred Wilson his *Luftwaffe* wings as a token of his appreciation.

Hospitalisation preceded internment, first in England and then in Canada. They counted themselves lucky – they had made history by being the first POWs to be captured on English soil and they were alive. The two airmen had been in their boat for forty-three hours, without food or water, and had suffered hypothermia and frostbite.

'Cowboy' Blatchford suffered a similar fate to these two German pilots in May 1943 when he was forced to ditch forty miles off the coast in the North Sea after being shot down. He did not survive.

THE NAVY CRIES FOR HELP

Unknown to us, on 14 October 1939 a German U-boat had managed to get into the heavily protected naval anchorage at Scapa Flow, with the result that the *Royal Oak* was sunk with a heavy loss of life. Then on 17 October a small force of bombers had raided the area, slightly damaging the old *Iron Duke*. One bomber was shot down.

With these events unknown to us we went to 'bed' at dispersal without seeing our families on 17 October. The night was no more restful than usual; sleep under such conditions in the tents was nearly always fitful, and after the events of the day, sleep became even more difficult. Long before dawn we were roused by the Flight Commander, who should have been sleeping in the mess that night – we were to collect our small kit, towel, soap, toothbrush and shaving tackle from our quarters and be ready to fly to Wick (the nearest aerodrome to Scapa Flow) at first light! The Royal Navy had asked for fighter protection. No single person outside the squadron aircrew were to be told of our move or destination. All we could say to our families was, 'Goodbye and see you soon', but how soon we didn't know, although two days was mentioned.

We were warned that Wick was 'dry', and we were urged to take some liquid sustenance with us. This was difficult because of the limited luggage compartment in the Spitfire. With judicious stowage of shaving kit and toothbrush in various pockets, some room was left for a small bottle of Scotch. When we had got our kit and maps together, dawn began to break, but the visibility clamped down, and in fact we did not get off until the middle of the afternoon. This late start meant we would not reach Wick that day. So we stayed the night at Drem (east of Edinburgh) after refuelling. Radio silence was maintained throughout and visual signals only were used as we flew north in loose formation. The next morning we left Drem and one hour and ten minutes later we landed at Wick.

Accommodation for the pilots was provided in the Station Hotel, while the ground crew were comfortably billeted in the town. There appeared to be only a couple of Naval Blackburn Skuas at Wick, which was a bleak, half-built place with very few facilities, a most uninviting place, to say the least. A chief petty officer who met us on the tarmac said that a German reconnaissance plane had been over regularly at 10.00 a.m. and 2 p.m. every day, dropping a stick of bombs and then going home unmolested. Our CO went off immediately to see the senior Naval officer to offer to put up a standing patrol of two aircraft over Scapa Flow (about thirty miles away) during the hours of daylight. This was turned down flat by the Admiral. The Admiral had refused to allow any aeroplanes to fly over Scapa Flow, and said that if we flew over there we would be fired at! The CO suggested that surely the Navy gunners knew the difference between a Spitfire and a German bomber – the Admiral was adamant – an aeroplane was an aeroplane and the gunners had orders to shoot! The Navy certainly seemed to be very touchy, and obviously very trigger happy! So, there were no standing patrols and all we could do was to maintain a section at standby on the ground!

A tragic accident

Before we left Catterick we knew that there were no facilities for us at Wick, so arrangements were made for a Whitley bomber from Driffield to ferry up to us essential equipment and materials, including tool kits, starter trolleys and about 30,000 rounds of belted ammunition which would give us a full rearm for the squadron, blankets, a corporal armourer, a corporal rigger and a spare pilot, who was to be Sergeant Albert 'Bill' Harris.

We were expecting the Whitley to be with us by nightfall on 19 October, but it never arrived. We were shocked to hear that it had crashed on take-off at Catterick, killing all but the two corporals. Luckily for the rigger, who was an ex-air-gunner, he had volunteered to occupy the rear tail turret in case of air attack, and realising that a crash was imminent he jumped out just in time. The other corporal being inside the aircraft was badly injured but lived. We heard that the crash was caused by the very heavy starter trolleys not being secured well enough and sliding back into the rear of the fuselage just after take-off, so that the aeroplane climbed much too steeply and stalled.[5]

> Late in the day the crew of this aircraft were tasked to fly to Catterick, and from there to ferry a load of ammunition to Wick. After loading the stores, five passengers boarded the aircraft. Sgt Gaut selected the longest available take-off run that was available between the Great North Road and the River Swale, but when about half-way across the airfield the Whitley suddenly rose to about ten feet, followed by a near-vertical climb at full throttle. Eye witnesses state that the bomber stalled below a hundred feet, and dived nose first into the ground, exploding on impact. Miraculously two of the five passengers survived the impact. Before take-off Sgt Gaut had protested that the aircraft was overloaded with the three starter trolleys, and he had telephoned his home base at Driffield to complain, but he was overruled. Among those killed was Sgt Harris, a Spitfire pilot, who on the previous day had shared in the destruction of a Heinkel 111 twenty miles east of Whitby, Yorkshire. Those killed were Sgt H.J. Gaut (pilot), Plt Off R.A.M. Luckman, AC1 C. Paterson, AC1 J.B. Clark, Sgt A. Vincent (41 Squadron), Sgt A.H. Harris (41 Squadron) and AC1 H. Jones (41 Squadron). Sgt Gibbs and Cpl Jenkinson were injured. [Source: RAF Bomber Command Losses, W.R. Chorley and Graeme Carrott, 'Air North' Vol. 41 No. 6, June 2001]

Mrs Violet Harris saw the crash and the explosion of the plane from the kitchen window of their house in Catterick. A neighbour (Maisie Carr Lewty) came outside and apparently said to her, 'It's all right, Mrs Harris. It was a Whitley that exploded.' So as Bill was a Spitfire pilot, she was a little bit relieved, thinking Albert would not have been involved, but time passed, they heard nothing (Maisie lived next door), and then the Military Police came to the house to break the awful news.[6]

So there we were, on a half-built aerodrome without the starter trolleys, tools and ammunition to make our stay more acceptable. While we could start the engines once or twice in emergency on the aircraft batteries, we had to find an alternative. So a tour of the local garages was made to commandeer all the car batteries we could find. Linking these together with twisted strands of copper wire we managed to produce a makeshift starter unit. One other innovation was to produce slip stones from selected pebbles, and after smoothing down a flat surface we could use these to deburr the gun mechanisms and keep them working in good order.

Although we told no one of our move to Wick, and maintained radio silence throughout the flight north, we learned on our arrival that our move was known in the village of Wick the day before we arrived – so much for security and intelligence! There seems little doubt that the Germans knew of our movements, too, because their twice-daily bombing sorties over Scapa Flow ceased immediately we arrived at Wick and began again when we left some six days later! By this time the fleet had been moved into a safer anchorage on the west coast of Scotland.

So our anticipated stay of two days at a cold, bleak and uncomfortable Wick turned out to be nearly a week. It was a disastrous event for the squadron, and we were glad to get home again, for we flew only once or twice on air tests and one false alarm. However, I suppose our presence saved the fleet from further attacks.

Wick turned out not to be 'dry', and the bottles of Scotch were never opened until we stopped at Drem on the return journey to refuel. There we shared the twelve bottles with another friendly Spitfire squadron. The final leg of the journey was a bit erratic due to the effects of the Scotch, but we managed to stay in sight of one another. Our arrival and landing at Catterick was later described as a bit 'uncontrolled'.

On returning home to my wife, Elsie, and our home in the married quarters at Catterick, I discovered that the news of our shooting down the first enemy aircraft by the squadron (and the RAF – not counting the RAuxAF) had become common knowledge on the station, and of course Elsie came to know of it that way. She thought I should have told her, but of course I didn't really have the opportunity before we left so hurriedly for Wick.

Soon after this the Tannoy public address system was installed throughout the station, including the dispersal points and the married quarters. This allowed the families to hear the 'scramble' orders given to us at readiness and thus enabled the families to be given any air raid warnings that came through, and it also let the family of a pilot know that he was being ordered off on an interception. Whether this was good to know or not was debatable.

'POOKY'S' NIGHT CRASH

The Spitfire was a difficult aircraft to fly at night. The long nose obscured forward vision, and with short exhaust stubs any attempt to peer forward alongside the nose was rewarded with a glare of flame. Take-off and the circuit had to be executed totally on instruments. This was quite a challenge for new pilots without experience of night-flying. George Bennions criticised the practice of sending inexperienced pilots on pitch-black night-flying flights without first some familiarisation in moonlight or dusk conditions. George's suggestions were adopted with some reluctance.[7]

At about this time during a night-flying session, a young Canadian officer from Niagara Falls, nicknamed 'Pooky' Overall, took off into a dark night sky and after climbing to about five hundred feet he started a turn to the right. This turn, intended to bring him downwind for an approach and landing, continued and developed into a gentler diving turn and he crashed into a house on the north side of the village about a quarter of a mile away. He was killed outright, and by coincidence the house concerned belonged to another pilot in his flight ('A') named Flt Sgt Bennions. 'Pooky' was an excellent pilot and it was judged unlikely that he had omitted to check the tightness of the friction nut on the throttle quadrant which prevents the throttle from sliding back unnoticed to the closed position.

The cause of the accident was not obvious, but speculation seemed to favour a failure of the primary instruments, the artificial horizon which on a black night when the natural horizon was not visible would easily mislead the pilot. The blackout of the domestic lights of the village and camp and the restricted light from the hooded flares would have been of no assistance.

However, I did have another thought which I felt might be investigated. It came from having watched several daylight take-offs where there appeared to be some venting of glycol coolant from the header tank overflow, which was situated just above the exhaust stubs of Numbers 3 and 4 cylinders on the starboard side. One could see long plumes of the whitish vapour stream past the cockpit, especially if the aircraft bounced a lot during the take-off run. I thought that if 'Pooky's' aircraft that night had had a bad case of this venting, the vapour might have entered the cockpit (since one always took off and landed with the hood open) and made the reading of the instruments that much more difficult, if not impossible. I tested one of the aircraft that I had noticed doing this, and found that bouncing did cause the glycol to escape and that it did tend to enter and swirl around the cockpit. Looking at the overflow vent when on the ground, one could see that its position relative to the engine cowling could well be causing a suction or vacuum at the outlet of the pipe. By trial and error I found that by making the pipe protrude outside the cowling and by arranging it so that it faced forwards slightly the venting ceased altogether, but of course it did not prevent venting because of any excess pressure in the header tank.

When Mrs Overall had been told of the crash and of the lucky escape of the occupants of the house, she invited the children to travel to Niagara Falls in Canada and stay with her for the duration of the war. The Canadian Government were very considerate and paid for the two fares: a touching end to 'Pooky's' death.

GREMLINS

During one rather long night trip I had my first experience of 'gremlins'. I was flying quite straight and level when I felt the control column, which I was holding in my right hand, shake quite violently from side to side – just as if someone was moving the ailerons up and down, which the ground crew would do to attract a pilot's attention when running an engine up before taxiing out. When I felt this quite sharp shaking of the control I instinctively looked out to the port wingtip – just as I would if on the ground. There was nothing there, of course, and the phenomenon stopped just as quickly as it started. We never found any satisfactory explanation for this peculiar happening, although on subsequent trips I found that it always occurred at a particular speed, but once one had got used to it one ceased to be concerned, and of course the 'gremlins' got the blame!

November and December 1939 produced no real operational activity. The few patrols that were ordered came to naught either because there was nothing to intercept, except perhaps seagulls, or because the plots turned out to be friendly aircraft. At this time the system of notification of friendly aircraft movements had not been fully developed, and sometimes, of course, our own returning bombers and reconnaissance aircraft, perhaps with damaged radio and navigation equipment, got off track, sometimes getting lost, and were necessarily treated as hostile until identified visually. So once again most of our occasional trips were devoted to training exercises, either for ourselves or for the anti-aircraft guns. Now and again we were allowed to 'let our hair down' a bit by 'beating up' the more remote gun sites, such as at Danby Beacon on the Cleveland Hills.

The first three months of 1940 were equally quiet, for I was ordered off on interceptions only four times, again to no purpose. However, there was no relaxation in our readiness. Flights of aircrew, ground crew and aircraft had to be ready, day or night, and at all times. Even in bad weather when conditions were almost impossible to fly safely we had to remain ready. There were many long hours of waiting and thinking. One read books and played cards until one was sick of both. Boredom was the immediate enemy, and sleep was often the result. We had one young pilot officer who became so irritable, angry and tensed up that he did nothing but pace up and down by himself; he was almost a nervous wreck. Another pilot went down with an ulcer.

Activities in January 1940 included night-flying practice, instrument flying practice (with a safety pilot in another Spitfire flying alongside), many uneventful coastal patrols, battle drills and climbs. 'Wally' Wallens was unfortunate to hit a concrete mixer on landing his Spitfire on 25 January 1940. February 1940 saw similar flying duties, including convoy patrols, experiments in attack procedure, low-flying attack practice and instrument flying. The weather was not conducive to flying, and only about twelve hours were achieved. There was plenty of snow on the ground, which made things tricky during taxiing, take-offs and landing. Indeed Bill Stapleton hit a pile of snow on the end of the runway and his Spitfire was a write-off. In March 1940 there more convoy patrols, defensive patrols, air frame and engine tests following a rebuild, night-flying, and some testing of cine-camera gun equipment.

'Buck' Ryan taxied out in a cloud of snow and missed the intersection between the perimeter taxiway and the runway. He opened his throttle to half power for take-off before he realised he was still on the perimeter taxi and not on the runway. A few unsuspecting airmen walking down the perimeter track were horrified to see a Spitfire hurtling towards them at full gallop, and they had to dive head first into the snow bank.

Landing on packed snow in brilliant sunshine was not easy. The reflection or glare from the glassy surface made height judgement difficult. There was the risk of either flying into the deck or holding off too high – both usually resulted in a heavy landing.

We became accustomed to our existence at dispersal either in tents or in wooden huts as we continued with more scrambles, convoy patrols and various training exercises. We made good friends with most men, especially those who hade been in 41 Squadron a long while. We were all aware of each other's abilities, limitations and strength of purpose. We were united and confined in our small world of a fighter squadron waiting for more action. Our common fear was that we might not 'put up a good show' or 'let the side down' or make a 'bloody fool of oneself'. All of us knew we might come to a violent death – we had seen it already. But worst of all was the fear being crippled or of suffering with burns.

Life expectancy in a fighter squadron was eighty-four hours, compared to eight weeks in the 1914–18 war. Fate would decide whether it was my turn tomorrow or the next day.

'WIMPEY'. MASCOT OF 41 SQUADRON IN 1939

It seemed the custom for squadrons to have a mascot, and it wasn't long before a rather ugly white bull terrier appeared on the strength of 'A' Flight. His name was J. Wellington Wimpey! Wimpey had the tip of one ear missing and was a bit of a trouble-maker. Once he relieved himself on the AOC's hat, which had fallen off the coat peg. The airmen used to play games with Wimpey and feed him tit-bits, but he had a reputation for biting if the fooling around got a bit too rough. He also chased some sheep on a neighbouring farm. He wasn't a very friendly character, and after a short while he disappeared south to another squadron when his owner was posted to take over a flight. This dog has appeared in sundry photographs of squadron aircraft, and one I particularly remember is where he was perched on the tailplane of a Hurricane. I am not sure if he came back to 41, but 'Wally' Wallens reckons that 'Wimpey' ended up with the farmer who looked after him and made sure he got plenty of exercise and not too many tit-bits.

CONVOY PATROLS

Increased activity came our way through the introduction of convoy patrols. Coastal shipping was now being shepherded to sail in small convoys to provide some degree of protection against air attack. The 'hit and run' raider had become a threat to this shipping and had been known to attack even small fishing boats. Except in very bad flying weather we provided a pair of aircraft to escort these convoys and to be in a position to defend them should raiders pop up unexpectedly. We had to be careful to show ourselves in a tactful way to the ships so that they would not mistake us for the enemy, and at the same time not get too close to them. They all had some form of armament, usually a Lewis gun, and the crews were keen to preserve their skins – who wouldn't be a little trigger happy in their shoes? Our area of duty for these convoy patrols was usually between Scarborough and Hartlepool. Later on, instead of wasting a lot of aircraft hours on these patrols, we maintained a section of three at readiness at a 'forward base'. This was on a small grass aerodrome at Greatham, just north-east of Middlesbrough, near Hartlepool. At the south end of the field, I remember, was a Cerebos salt factory! The north/south grass runway was 2,000 yards and the other two grass runways, east/west and north-east/south-west, were 1,600 yards each. There were ten hardstandings around the perimeter. There were no hangars, maintenance or mess facilities – just a single wooden hut which served as flying control office and crew room. At a busy time there might be thirty-six officers, 182 NCOs and 446 other ranks on duty at Greatham. There was no fuel at the airfield, which meant that aircraft returning after a long patrol could not land at Greatham. With no overnight accommodation, any pilots forced down by bad weather had to leave their machines and be driven back to Catterick for the night. There were no fire and rescue facilities, which worried a few pilots. A

Blenheim Mark I (L6709) from 219 Squadron crashed on landing after an engine failed during the approach on 24 March 1940, and was written off.[8]

The field next to the airfield yielded a good crop of mushrooms, and these were often collected after negotiating the rolls of defensive barbed wire. The readiness section used to go over to Greatham at dawn, there were changes of section at midday and at tea time, and the last shift of the day arrived back at Catterick at dusk. A direct 'scramble' telephone was installed and the arrangement was very successful. It was from Greatham that I was to make a 'copy book' interception against a bomber which had been attacking coastal shipping and fishermen, on 21 August 1940.

'GUIZZY'

One of the interesting characters we had at Catterick early in 1940 was Pilot Officer the Lord Guisborough, Master of Fox Hounds of the Cleveland Hunt and an ex-prisoner of war of WWI. He came to us in the role of assistant intelligence officer. 'Guizzy' was a great sport and very keen to get his own back on the Germans for the pretty rotten time they gave him as a prisoner in WWI. Armed with his constant companion, a .45 Colt. and equipped with gas mask and gas cape, battle bowler and a dispatch rider's satchel, he spent most of his time pedalling his Mark I service bicycle between the intelligence office in the station headquarters and the dispersal points. He took his job most seriously and accepted the many jokes played on him by the younger aircrew officers with much patience and good humour.

One evening (26 April 1940) at dusk, when I was leading Green Section home from Greatham, my Number Two, Sgt Howitt (a Grantham lad) had the misfortune to strike the landing approach indicator with his undercarriage as he landed. He turned over but fortunately was not hurt; however, his machine needed some attention!

It was our practice on these occasions to form line astern and land individually on the right-hand side of the flare-path, but Howitt disobeyed my landing instructions and landed on the left-hand side of the flares. Anyway, he must have been careless, as the approach indicator was easily visible some yards downwind of the first flare and almost in line with it. This indicator was not large – about three feet long by a foot wide and not more than one and half feet high. The indicator projected a beam of light at an angle of three degrees in the direction of landing aircraft. The beam of light was split into three colours horizontally – yellow at the top, green in the middle and red at the bottom, the indications to the pilot being yellow – 'too high', green – 'correct' and red – 'too low'.

There had been one or two other non-operational accidents in the group. My flight commander landed my Spitfire aircraft 'wheels up'. It was soon after Howitt's altercation with the landing approach indicator that the AOC visited all the stations to read the 'Riot Act' to us all!

CONSOLIDATED RATION ALLOWANCE (CRA)

All married airmen who were entitled to a paid ration allowance were given an additional 'consolidated ration allowance' of about thirty shillings per quarter to cover the cost of miscellaneous items such as salt, pepper and mustard, which couldn't very well be issued. This allowance was authorised by an entry in the station's PORs (personnel occurrence reports) along with other entitlements. Normally the wives of the airmen did not have access to PORs and only knew this extra allowance by the letter CRA. Taking advantage of this fact, it was said that some airmen explained to their wives that CRA stood for cycle repair allowance, thus enabling them to pocket the extra cash for themselves and not to put it into the housekeeping purse!

A COMMISSION

As one might gather from my last description of the convoy patrols, by this time I had been elevated to the dizzy height of section leader, and usually flew as Green Leader or Green One. Then on 1 April 1940 I was informed that I was to be commissioned in the rank of pilot officer. Flt Sgt 'Benny' Bennions was also given a commission. Another chum, Flt Sgt Jimmy Sayers, should have been commissioned too, but he was often unwell with a duodenal ulcer and was therefore not accepted. Later on in 1942 when I landed at Catterick from Central Flying School (CFS) on my way to Silloth I found that Jimmy had ended up as the barrack warden (in charge of the domestic stores).

Benny and I were called up to HQ 13 Group for an interview with the AOC, who was none other than Air Vice-Marshal R.E. Saul,[9] my old CO at Old Sarum, and incidentally the brother of the Capt Saul who flew with Charles Kingsford-Smith across the Atlantic in *Southern Cross*. My interview was rather an uncomfortable one, for it was brief and consisted mainly of, 'You were mixed up in that Heinkel affair, weren't you?' Little else was discussed, and knowing 'Dickie' Saul of old I had no intention of trying to find out what he was getting at, nor was I keen to prolong the interview. He was still the short-tempered and rather unsociable Irishman that we knew at Old Sarum. I naturally wondered whether my commission would suffer as a result of this interview, but it did not do so.

On reflection I can only think that what the AOC objected to 'in that Heinkel affair' was my action as a number two breaking away and taking the lead in the attack, but this is what we had agreed to do in the squadron, and in that particular case the Heinkel would certainly have got away if I had not done so.

So it was goodbye to crowns and stripes and airmen's married quarters (AMQs). I collected my uniform allowance of £40 and went to the locally approved tailor in Northallerton. This princely sum provided me with a complete uniform, tailored by Simpsons of Piccadilly, consisting of tunic, trousers, two shirts and collars, cap, greatcoat and raincoat, gloves and shoes, with sufficient cash left over to provide a new pair of Wellington boots and a large leather suitcase. From the station stores I was issued with an officer's camp kit, which, in addition to the folding bed with three blankets, contained a canvas wash-bowl, canvas folding bath and a bucket! Finally, having packed up the married quarter and taken Elsie with our household belongings to Darlington, to her parents' home, at 49 Brook Terrace, I went to live in the officers' mess.

No. 219 Squadron and 'Batchy' Atcherley

When No. 219 Squadron was formed at Catterick following the departure of No. 26 Squadron to France, it was a squadron without aircraft. The night-fighter Bristol Blenheims were not available, so 'Batchy' Atcherley, the CO, managed to get six Miles Magisters for the pilots to fly in the meantime – in his opinion it was quite unthinkable for a flying squadron not to have a single aircraft, even for a few weeks. Furthermore, a night-flying squadron must have aeroplanes equipped for night-flying! The Magisters were not so equipped. But Batchy was not to be thwarted: he very quickly got the necessary navigation lamps from a civilian pal at Histon. These lamps were the three colours in one lamp identical to that he had fitted to his Avian at Farnborough. Accumulators were installed, and very soon night-flying began in earnest.

'TOTEM-POLES'

It was at this time that 'Batchy' produced his 'totem-pole' idea of marking the night landing area. This was to have poles about ten or twelve feet high fitted with electric lights about a foot apart down one side. The poles were mobile and stood on wooden bases. They were placed at either end of the take-off and landing run, with the lights facing the pilot as he took off and landed. At first only two totem-poles were used, but later four were used, so that the width as well as the length of the area was marked. Later still the lights on the poles were fitted with hoods to limit the vision of them to a pilot approaching to land, and, of course, during take-off and landing. The idea was very successful.

'BATCHY'S' DAILY DOSE

From the moment the first Magister arrived at Catterick, 'Batchy' flew every day, whatever the weather. His take-off run would begin from the tarmac, if not from the hangar doors – irrespective of the wind direction! His flying was a tonic to watch.

Thick mist or even fog was no deterrent to 'Batchy', and on such occasions he would not have to bother about other aircraft in the air – because there weren't any in such weather. On one such occasion I saw his take-off from the hangar door across the tarmac, fastening his helmet as he went. Within a hundred yards he was out of sight in the thick mist and climbing up over the aerodrome. We could hear him circling round above but could see nothing at all. About ten minutes later we heard him throttle back to glide down. Then out of the mist he appeared, coming in to land between the two hangars from where he took off. He certainly could not have seen the hangars or the ground before he began his landing approach, but he was really 'spot on' and finished his landing without using his engine, ending up not many yards from the tarmac. He did this type of short landing once too often, for on one occasion he brought down some telephone and public address cables which were stretched between the two hangars!

Crazy flying

One morning when there were several inches of snow on the ground, 'Batchy' delighted the onlookers by doing his crazy flying act on the aerodrome. Some said he was trying to write his name in the snow with his wingtip – one could certainly see the snow being churned up by the wingtip, and it was much to the disgust of the Flight Sergeant that one of the Magister's wingtips had to be replaced!

The first Blenheim

One new black-painted Blenheim duly arrived and created much interest with its sinister looking radar aerials on its wings. But much to 'Batchy's' disappointment it didn't have its complement of four Browning guns. So, not to be put off by this deficiency, 'Batchy' phoned a pal at Eastchurch (an armament station) and asked if he had any guns to spare. 'Yes,' was the reply, 'what do you want for four?' 'A case of champagne!' 'Right.' The outcome of this brief conversation was that a case of champagne went to Eastchurch and the necessary guns arrived at Catterick. Within hours there was a fully armed Blenheim on patrol from Catterick for the first time.

The day after the raid on the Firth of Forth, 'Batchy' got permission to do a sector reconnaissance in the Blenheim. In the operations room the controller kept in touch by radio and plotted 'Batchy'. He was heading north towards the Scottish sector, and when he was almost on the boundary the controller warned him that he should turn back to keep in his own sector. There was no reply. The plot continued north, obviously heading for the Firth of

Forth. The controller called again and asked 'Batchy' if he could hear him. 'Yes', said 'Batchy'. The controller thought he was going to win at last, and again explained the need to turn back, and instructed him to do so immediately. Back came 'Batchy': 'I'm sorry, old boy, I'm afraid I can't hear you!' So keen was 'Batchy' for action that when he had several Blenheims serviceable for operation he badgered the AOC to let him take his aircraft on intruder raids against Sylt and other targets across the North Sea. His plea was frowned upon and refused.

As a man of great drive, ingenuity and personality, 'Batchy' had a unique quality of turning up with something or some act to suit the occasion and to keep things going in a lively fashion, and many tales could be told to illustrate this character. *A Pride of Unicorns*, the biography of the Atcherley twins, contains many such stories. A few others not in the book are worth describing here.

One of 'Batchy's' airmen, who was not a service driver, saw that a tractor towing a petrol bowser needed moving to get on with the refuelling. He used his initiative and drove the tractor himself as the proper driver was not around. In doing this he collided with another vehicle and damaged one of the headlamps. As it was not an emergency and the damage had to be accounted for, the airman was placed on a Form 252 and charged with causing damage to the vehicle. Appearing before 'Batchy', the airman was necessarily found guilty and would have to pay something at least towards the cost of the damage. In true 'Batchy' fashion for showing initiative and making an effort to help, he gave the airman an admonishment, which meant that no entry would be put on his service sheet, and ordered him to pay £1. After the airman had been marched out of the office, 'Batchy' called back the Flight Sergeant, gave him a £1 note and told him to give it to the airman.

In the mess 'Batchy' was inclined to play jokes on all and sundry and to be somewhat eccentric. Sitting opposite him one day at lunch, I saw him play a trick on a young officer who was sitting next to him. The officer had got up from his chair to go to the buffet table, and while he was gone 'Batchy' poured a little water into the centre of the sagging leather seat of the vacant chair. The reaction of the young officer can well be imagined when he sat down again with the iced water soaking through his trousers and pants. He jumped up sharply and looked at his chair and then at Batchy with an air of indignation. 'Batchy' turned to look at the young chap with deep innocence on his face, then looked at the chair and remarked sharply, with disgust now written all over his face, 'Do you have to do that here?'

At one time both squadrons were confined to camp to be operationally available, but there was no activity. This went on for some days, and as 219 didn't do day operations they got no activity at all and they were very bored indeed. Before this period was over 'Batchy' declared that if he couldn't go out to play golf he would play inside, and inside it was – in the mess! The anteroom was the course and the ashtrays were the balls. When he had let off sufficient steam he gave the mess secretary a cheque to make good the damage!

PROMOTION

It wasn't long before 'Batchy's' promotion to wing commander came through, and with it a signal of congratulation from the Chief of Air Staff, Sir Cyril Newall. The promotion didn't suit 'Batchy' in the least, and when I had the opportunity of congratulating him he remarked that it would mean that he wouldn't be able to fly so much. He promptly replied to the CAS's signal with a long letter giving all the reasons why he should not be promoted. But that made no difference and he was posted to Drem as the station commander.

At Drem it was not long before 'Batchy' had developed his idea on aerodrome lights for night-flying, and so emerged the Drem Airfield Lighting System. This was based on his 'totem-pole' idea, with large paraffin flares situated some distance from the airfield upwind and downwind, with some additional guiding lights on the airfield itself. The whole idea was to help the pilot to orient himself in relation to the 'totem-poles', which, since these were hooded and restricted, were difficult to see. Variations of this basic system were evolved until we got what amounted to the full airfield lighting virtually as it is today – more like Piccadilly Circus!

One incident, typical of Batchy, was recounted to me by an officer who was serving at Drem with him. There were too many cars being parked at night, particularly in front of the officers' mess, and 'Batchy' issued an order that no car should be parked there. One dark and pouring-wet night this officer was walking to the mess when he saw in the dim light a car at the main entrance, with a figure bending down at one of the rear wheels. On getting a closer look he saw that it was 'Batchy' in his dressing gown! The officer asked if he could help. 'Yes,' said Batchy, 'the front wheel – quick!' The officer went to the front wheel and saw that it was fully inflated, and said so to 'Batchy', who snapped back, 'I know it is, let the bloody thing down!' The owner of the car was being taught a lesson he wouldn't forget in a hurry!

AN ATTEMPT TO ESCAPE

A visiting Tiger Moth landed with minor engine trouble and the flight sergeant of the duty flight was to have a look at it. One of the first things to be checked were the contact-breakers of the two magnetos, so the contact-breaker covers were removed. Then in order to see if the breaker points were opening correctly and had the right gap, the Flight Sergeant got another airman to turn over the propeller slowly while he watched the contact-breakers. There was nothing wrong or strange in this, but suddenly the attention of all on the tarmac was drawn to the noise of the Tiger's engine coming to life and revving up; but not only that, for the Tiger was careering drunkenly away from the tarmac out onto the aerodrome – the Flight Sergeant and his helpers tearing after it. With no one at the helm the Tiger was steering an erratic course, and it seemed unlikely to get airborne. However, as it happened the machine began a gradual turn to the left, so giving the pursuers a chance to take a short cut to intercept it. This they managed to do, and grabbing the port wingtip to swing the machine round in a tighter circle they eventually brought it to a standstill. It was a very red-faced and breathless Flight Sergeant who was very thankful indeed that no real damage had been done.

The moral of this episode is never to check the contact-breakers of an engine fitted with an impulse starter by turning the propeller forwards, because with the contact-breaker cover removed the magneto is switched on and will certainly ignite any mixture in the cylinders, especially in a warm engine, however slowly the engine is turned! Always turn the engine backwards. And in this particular case the fuel had been left turned on and the throttle must have been slightly open!

THE 'DITCHING' OF THE FIRST SPITFIRE

In particularly bad weather we used to send off single aircraft
against any reported raids. On this occasion, on 3 April 1940,
there was heavy low cloud at about three hundred feet above sea
level, and rain. We were told that fishing boats were being
attacked off the Saltburn coast. At 12.21 p.m. Flg Off Norman
Ryder of 'A' Flight (who was the top pupil on my junior course at
Thornaby SFTS) was sent off from Greatham to try to deal with
the raider. He managed to find his target seventeen minutes later,
in spite of the really awful conditions, and went into the attack.
Norman Ryder intercepted a Heinkel 111K (1H + AC) of *Stab* II/
KG 26[10] fifteen miles north-east of Whitby and four miles off the
coast. The Heinkel was carrying out an armed reconnaissance
sortie and had just carried out an attack on a small convoy of
fishing vessels. A bomb had been dropped onto the ships and the
Heinkel had received some fire from the ships. The port engine
had been hit, disabling the electrics, a large hole in the port wing
created drag, and steering was most difficult, with a constant drift
to port despite full, opposite rudder trim and pumping (by hand)
fuel from the port wing tanks to those in the starboard wing. The
Heinkel was in trouble and only about two hundred feet above
the sea. Norman Ryder's interception was fast, and he had to slow
down and circle before attacking from astern while in a left-hand
turn. Concentrating his fire on the good engine of the Heinkel, a
six-second burst from the eight Browning machine-guns struck
the Heinkel's starboard engine and main plane. The Heinkel
attempted to climb but with reduced power this was not possible.
Norman broke away left and returned to attack. As he did so he
saw the Heinkel's starboard engine emitting smoke and some
flame. Norman refrained from firing and instead positioned
himself to the starboard side of the Heinkel and watched it
descend to the sea. Norman's Spitfire received two hits during the
engagement, and these had gone almost unnoticed apart from
two large bangs under the engine.

The Heinkel ditched into the North Sea in a seven-foot swell,
and the five crew de-planed quickly before it sank. The dinghy
was useless as it was riddled with bullet holes. Norman circled
the German crew and saluted, but Alfred Bachle noticed that the
Spitfire was trailing white smoke or fluid. The German crew were

picked up by the *Silver Line*, one of the fishing vessels. The German crew surrendered their pistols and Hans Hefele said, 'Make for England, we never wanted to fight you anyway.'

Norman Ryder made a beeline course for home, and immediately saw his oil temperature was rising quickly. He radioed Control that he was in trouble with the cockpit filling up with hot oil fumes. Catterick Control spelled out the options: make for land, bale out or ditch. Norman found these obvious statements most unhelpful. With low cloud preventing a safe climb for a bale-out and a high risk of engine failure before reaching the coast, Norman decided to ditch the Spitfire. The trawler *Alaska* was spotted, and Ryder decided to circle this and ditch close by if possible. Before this excellent plan could be executed, and when he was about fifty feet above the waves and half a mile from the trawler, Norman had just selected the flaps in the 'down' position to reduce the landing speed and was just opening the hood when the Rolls-Royce engine seized solid. The Spitfire ploughed into a seven-foot wall of water after it lost flying speed with a loud crash. Norman was knocked unconscious by the impact. The Spitfire sank immediately at a steep angle. As the water turned from a light green to a much darker hue Norman came to and released his straps and stood on the seat to float free. Nothing happened. His parachute was snagged on the hood. Norman climbed back into the cockpit and finally released his parachute, but now the water was very dark. His lungs were almost busting for lack of air, and he told me later that he had almost decided to end his agony by inhaling sea-water. When he managed to get free, with the parachute still attached, progress to the surface was slow. However, he found that he was sinking again, and realising that he still had his parachute on and thinking that the weight of it was pulling him down, he released it. To his surprise the freed parachute shot up to the surface of the sea and he began to sink further – the parachute was more effective than his Mae West! Fortunately he managed to grab the straps of his parachute and pull himself up to the surface again. Once on the surface he found that his Mae West had not inflated and that his saturated clothes were too heavy to ride the swell. Most of the waves were breaking over his head. Quickly realising the benefit of the parachute, Norman grasped it and hung on for all he could. Eventually the *Alaska* came alongside and he was hauled aboard.

The Heinkel had managed to put a single bullet through Norman's oil cooler. This may have been a lucky shot, for he knew nothing of it until his engine failed due to oil shortage and overheating. This was the very first time a Spitfire had been landed in the sea, and naturally we had been given no advice on how it would behave. With the flaps in the 'down' position the machine immediately nosed down into the sea and sank almost vertically. According to the report, fortunately possible because Norman survived, the aircraft did not float at all but went straight down, with the greenish colour of the sea rapidly becoming darker and darker as he struggled to get out of the cockpit.

Norman Ryder's Spitfire was the first one that the *Luftwaffe* had managed to shoot down. Back at Catterick we were anxiously waiting for news. Norman was one of the nicest chaps I have ever met, and one of the better officers and more popular members of the squadron. After what seemed to be many hours, but was not more than a couple at the most, we heard that he had been picked up and was well except for sea sickness and exposure. The next day he was back with us, having made a very detailed and valuable report on the behaviour of a Spitfire when ditched. He was awarded the DFC. No doubt the very bad weather in which he went out was also taken into account. This being the squadron's first decoration, we duly celebrated in the usual way.

Norman Ryder's more recent claim to public notice was when he took part in the race from Paris to the Marble Arch as a group captain, flying by Hawker Hunter, helicopter and finally by motorcycle. This was in the late 1960s.

NOTES

1. Each individual aircraft maintained its service identity, irrespective of which squadron or duty it was assigned to by carrying a manufacturer's plate with a five-figure alphanumeric serial number. For the Battle of Britain period, these serials consisted of an individual letter followed by four numbers. In most cases, but not all, this serial was stencilled on the rear fuselage.
2. Full throttle up to the gate, or stop, on the quadrant, but not engaging the supercharger.
3. Information from Bill Norman, author of *Luftwaffe over the North*.

4. A *Gruppe* of three *Staffeln* formed the basic operational unit, with each *Staffel* linked administratively and operationally. Generally, three or more *Gruppen* formed a *Geschwader*.

5. RAF Records: On 18 October 1939, 41 Squadron was ordered to Wick, Caithness. The pilots took off with their twelve Spitfires, followed by the servicing party in a Whitley aircraft of 102 (Ceylon) Squadron, which was based at RAF Driffield. Pilot of the Whitley Mark III (K8996) was Sergeant Herbert 'Acker' Gaut. The crew of the Whitley included the second pilot Pilot Officer Reginald Luckman, the wireless operator AC2 Charles Peterson and an air gunner AC1 John Clark. The Whitley crashed shortly after take-off from Catterick. Aboard the plane were personnel from 41 Squadron, including Sergeant Pilot Albert Harris, Aircraftman 1st Class Horace Jones, Sergeant Arthur Vincent. These and four of the Whitley's crew were killed, while Sergeant D. Gibbs and Corporal Jenkinson were seriously injured. Gibbs did not return to the squadron from sick leave until 9 December 1939. [Source: 41 Squadron ORB, TNA Air 27/424]

6. Information from Eleanor Collins (formerly Harris).

7. Patrick Bishop, *Fighter Boys*.

8. Additional information from Graeme Carrott and 'Air North', Vol. 42, No. 2, February 2002.

9. Air Vice-Marshal Richard Saul had flown as an observer in the First World War and had won the DFC.

10. The Heinkel was commanded by *Gruppenkommandeur Oberstleutnant* Hans Hefele and crewed by *Leutnant* Rudolf Behnisch (pilot), *Leutnant* Georg Kempe (observer), *Unteroffizier* Albert Weber (radio operator) and *Unteroffizier* Alfred Bachle (mechanic).

CHAPTER 8

Dunkirk

On 28 May 1940 we were ordered to fly as a squadron to Hornchurch to take part in covering the Dunkirk evacuation.

The element of chance in meeting the enemy during defensive sorties was clearly evident to us. No. 41 Squadron flew ten sorties or patrols, and out of these ten I flew seven, due to a shortage of serviceable aircraft. During the seven patrols over Dunkirk I had only one glimpse of the enemy popping in and out of cloud some distance away. In contrast the other three patrols for the squadron were full of activity. For me, Dunkirk seemed a frustrating period. The weather was difficult, and the lack of good communications with other squadrons on patrol made matters worse. The length of the patrols was a problem, too, as it stretched the economical engine handling of the Spitfire to the limit, the fuel capacity being only 85 gallons (386 litres).

The reference to other squadrons on patrol and poor communication is of particular interest, and this difficulty fuelled the controversial disagreement between Air Vice-Marshal Park and Leigh-Mallory later that summer. It is not widely known that at this period three or four squadrons were sent, on occasion, from different stations to patrol the same section of the French coast simultaneously. Because they were equipped with TR9D HF radio,[1] which only had one channel, they each had to use a different frequency and could not inter-communicate. This was a powerful argument in favour of Park.[2] Almost immediately after a short briefing I took off to patrol the Dunkirk beaches. On this occasion I was flying a Mk I Spitfire, L5949, the weather over the Channel was clear and one could see the billowing black smoke from the burning fires miles away. There were ships and

76

boats of all sizes dotted all over the area. Lying on its side and half submerged was what we were told was a hospital ship. Our job was to keep off the incoming aircraft, so being on the look-out for them we were not able to see much of the soldiers on the beaches. We were airborne for just over one and a half hours, but made no contact with the enemy. The weather over France seemed bad, so this may have been the reason for the lack of activity at this time. During our stay at Hornchurch we did ten patrols over the beaches, but as we had more pilots than aircraft we flew on a roster, which limited me to only seven patrols.

The next day, 29 May 1940, I was over the beaches again. The weather was not so good this time, and we saw only one aircraft, which promptly dived into cloud before we got near it. It looked like a Lysander, but this was not likely as there were few about at that time. We did get some flak but no harm was done. This trip lasted two hours and forty minutes, a record for Spitfires without extra tanks, and we had to land at Gravesend for fuel. It was here that we came across Douglas Bader, who was the CO of 242 Hurricane Squadron. After refuelling we went back to Manston on standby, from where we did one short trip before going back to Hornchurch.

Because we were flying Spitfires our patrols over the beaches were to give high cover, leaving the Hurricanes to operate at low level. On 30 and 31 May 1940 I did trips of one hour fifty and one hour fifty-five respectively, and again we saw nothing at altitude. There was another trip for me as Green Leader on 21 June 1940, which lasted two hours and twenty minutes. Finally, it was decided that we would operate at wing strength instead of as a squadron, but this was not very successful since the squadrons making up the wing had to operate on different radio frequencies and therefore could not keep in touch with each other. My first wing patrol was on 3 June 1940, and I was Green Leader again; this was a trip of two hours and twenty minutes.

My final patrol over Dunkirk, again in wing strength, was on 4 June 1940. We were awakened very early, the weather was bad and flying looked doubtful. However, the squadron received a telegram from Mr Churchill stating that the situation on the beaches was desperate and that 'if humanly possible' we were to go out over the beaches once more. This we did, taking off in the half light of a cloudy, dull dawn. Again we saw nothing at height, and after being in the air for two hours and twenty-five minutes I landed my section safely at Tangmere because the weather at Hornchurch was unfit. Several of our chaps ran out of fuel on this trip, and made forced landings at Manston and elsewhere. I think one was with wheels up somewhere just north of the Thames estuary.

As the luck of the draw would have it, the squadron got knocked about quite a bit on the three patrols that I did not fly on. We lost Flg Off Bill Legard on 1 June (missing) and Plt Off Bill Stapleton, who was later named as a POW. It was on one of these trips that our CO, Sqn Ldr 'Robin' Hood, having used up all his ammunition, saw a Ju 88 coming towards him at a lower altitude. He dived head on towards this aircraft, with the result that it also dived, to avoid the Spitfire, and crashed into the sea. On one of our early trips over the beaches, when 'Robin' Hood was asked by the ground station what the situation was, he replied, 'What a bloody fuck-up, nothing but shit and corruption!' How true!

During this stay at Hornchurch a flight commander of 74 Squadron, James Leathart, received the DSO for taking a Miles Master trainer over to an airfield in enemy-occupied territory somewhere south and behind Dunkirk, where he picked up his squadron commander, who had been shot down earlier. He was later promoted and took over 54 Squadron.

A new sergeant pilot attempted a take-off from Hornchurch and unfortunately failed to correct the incipient swing with opposite rudder. This swing is caused by the torque of the Merlin engine, and if not corrected can lead to an embarrassing or a dangerous situation. As the pilot opened the throttle to the take-off position the swing became more uncontrollable, and instead of throttling back and aborting the take-off he continued. Eventually he realised that his course at right angles to the runway was unwise – he was heading for one of the hangars – and he pulled back his throttle. As the Spitfire slowed down it rammed the wall of the hangar and entered a large office, where a warrant officer in charge of aircraft maintenance was busy at his desk. The wing of the Spitfire went past his head and the airscrew and nose embedded themselves in the back wall of the office. The pilot was uninjured but a little shocked at the mess. In a cloud of dust and plaster the WO shouted at the pilot, 'Next time you come into my bloody office, knock on the bloody door first.'[3]

On 8 June 1940 we returned to Catterick. On 18 June Frank Usmar joined the squadron. Frank had joined up while studying to be an accountant. When he arrived at Catterick railway station he was asked by a corporal if he was there as a replacement for the pilots lost over Dunkirk. The Spitfire was totally new to Frank. After three satisfactory practice flights he was considered competent on the Spitfire.[4]

OXYGEN FAILURE

It was the rule to turn on our oxygen supply when on the climb at about 8,000 feet, and this meant that a lack of oxygen could occur at altitude if we forgot to turn it on in the heat of the moment or if some fault had occurred in the supply, in which case the lack of oxygen might not be discovered until too late. These possibilities were reduced by a later rule to use oxygen from the word 'go', or in other words as soon as one was strapped in. This enabled the ground crew to check with the pilot that he was getting his oxygen correctly. However, before this new procedure was achieved there were one or two instances of anoxia in the squadron. The first was our 'A' Flight Commander, who passed out at high altitude while leading a battle flight. His companions in the formation saw him leave them suddenly by going into a tight loop and diving steeply towards the ground. They didn't expect to see him again, but he luckily came to at quite a low altitude, but just in time to pull out of the dive and land safely. Fortunately he was little the worse for his experience except that his eyes were badly bloodshot and he was black and blue around his eyes due to the bursting of small blood vessels.

My one and only experience of anoxia was due to a failure of the supply at a bayonet connection in the aircraft. I was leading my Green Section with two new pilots trying to intercept 'Weather Willie', a regular German visitor on weather reconnaissance off the coast of Durham. As this was the first operational scramble for my two companions, Plt Off Langley[5] and Sgt Usmar, and we would have to use as little RT as possible since we had found that these intruders were listening to our radio, I instructed them to watch me carefully and stick to me at a reasonable distance in open formation. The weather was fine and the visibility was reasonably good, and fortunately, as it happened, we didn't have to go above 19,000 feet, so the effect of my lack of oxygen was not abrupt. What I experienced was a gradual haziness, which I assumed to be worsening visibility – even thinking it seemed to be getting dark! I had vague visions of slight climbs and dives and eventually heard the order to return to base, and did so in a normal fashion, not realising fully what had been going on. My companions thought at first that my 'antics' were part of my efforts to exercise them in maintaining formation – fortunately my 'antics' were not too severe!

On this occasion I was lucky not to have had to go much higher, otherwise I might have passed out completely rather than becoming virtually drunk and semi-incapable, with little harm done except having missed 'Weather Willie' once again. His routine was usually a quick run-in, up or down the coast, and an even quicker run home again.

In retrospect these incidents, among others, caused us to appreciate the fact more fully that the Spitfire's fore-and-aft stability needed the controlling hand of the pilot to maintain a stable and safe flight. This characteristic was a design feature to provide the manoeuvrability required in a fighter – a stable aeroplane is not a very manoeuvrable one. The need for the elevator control to be fully trimmed to give the pilot the best chance of survival in such incidents became more obvious to us all – we had to learn by our mistakes.

Night operations and not much help!

Towards the end of June 1940, because a runway was being built at Catterick we had to send a section to Leeming for night readiness. The Blenheims of 219 Squadron had gone to Driffield and we were held in reserve to them. As usual at night, Spitfires would be sent off individually, with the flare-path limited to two dimly lit 'totem-poles' marking the direction of take-off and each end of the runway. We were allowed to sleep in our flying kit, but conditions were far from comfortable lying on the stone floor of the watch office with only a straw palliasse to provide some degree of comfort.

Although the chances of being sent off were slight, the night of 28 June 1940 brought an unusual amount of activity. Very early in the morning, at about half past three, when one's mental condition is usually pretty low, I was awakened and ordered off. It was very dark indeed and I think I must have got into the aircraft and started up almost by instinct, because I certainly did not feel at all awake. Taking off from alongside the first 'totem-pole', I headed for the other one in the black distance and staggered into the air, climbing north-east towards Middlesbrough. Bombs had just been dropped south-east of the town at 03.14 hours, damaging fourteen houses in the Grove Hill district and killing Middlesbrough's first air-raid victim – a Mrs Morley. Hutton Hall military camp at Guisborough was bombed, too, this time by four enemy aircraft – Guizzy's grouse moors might well be at stake!

I was sent out to sea off West Hartlepool at about 9,000 feet – the target was said to be some way ahead of me, so I had to get a move on to catch up, and opened up the throttle through the 'gate' to maximum boost, or to 'Buster', which was the code for maximum continuous operation – I could see nothing but the sparks and flares from the engine's open exhaust pipes just a yard or so in front of me.

I must have gone some seventy miles out when I lost RT contact with the controller, a WAAF. As I was getting no joy at all I turned back on a reciprocal heading – there seemed little purpose in going on. When I regained radio contact again I was sent out again more or less due east, with no better results. Having lost RT contact once more I came back again and once more was vectored out, this time about south-east. The target was said to be 'just in front', but there was nothing to be seen at all. I persevered for quite a while after I had lost RT contact for the third time, and then I turned back in the direction of home. The chances of an interception were absolutely nil, and I had been airborne for some fifty minutes and my fuel was getting low. When I managed to get RT contact again I was told to return to base. Naturally I requested a course to steer for base. After a short delay the controller asked me for my position! They were obviously not plotting me and had no idea where I was, and yet they had been, supposedly, con-trolling me onto a target! At this I blew my top and my patience was exhausted, having been chasing in and out over the sea for at least three-quarters of an hour; to be asked for my position was the last straw, and it was the height of ignorance and lack of understanding. My reply, I'm afraid, was, 'How the bloody hell do I know!' I suppose this was asking for it. Anyway, I got no further reply or help from the controller that night.

Using my imagination as to where I might be in relation to the coast, I set course due west, and after what seemed far too long and wondering whether my fuel would see me home, I was very relieved to be able to make out the faint outline of the coast ahead. And, thank goodness, a minute or so later I could just make out the shape of a small harbour in among the cliffs – it was Whitby! Now I knew I was all right, and one hour and ten minutes after take-off I landed at Leeming.

Later the next day I had to see the Station Commander regarding my language on the RT. Although I was officially 'on the mat', and might be reprimanded or disciplined, I left his office with his fullest sympathy.

BALLOON CHASING

The first half of July 1940 brought little operational activity, and I was even able to revert to my old job of instrument-flying training in the Magister. One of the pilots I took up was Plt Off 'Lockie', or 'Sawn off', Lock,[6] who later became a very high scorer[7] before he was killed. On 19 July 1940 I was sent off to shoot down a drifting barrage balloon that had floated across the aerodrome from west to east and was heading out to sea. I had to wait until it was over the sea, for obvious reasons, and the task proved more difficult than it appeared at first sight. It was not easy to judge the range accurately and the closing speed was quite high. The best result was obtained by using a 'hose pipe' technique – that is, aiming by watching the stream of bullets, as one might direct a hose pipe.

This was not very successful, although some hits were made and the balloon slowly deflated and lost height – no doubt it was in the water long before it reached the Dutch coast. At this time we had no incendiary ammunition, otherwise there might have been a more spectacular end to the balloon.

HORNCHURCH AGAIN

On 26 July 1940 we were on the way to Hornchurch once more, where we stayed just under two weeks. The main task was the protection of the convoys passing through the Channel. Being so close to the French coast they were easy prey for the German aircraft, and particularly the Ju 87 dive-bombers, which were being heavily protected by Me 109 fighters.

By this time the idea was to put a number of our fighters on standby at Manston, but although this arrangement put the fighters much nearer the convoys in case of a surprise attack, it was a double-edged arrangement. The distance to the convoys was so short that we inevitably arrived on the scene at a much lower altitude than the 109s, with the great disadvantage of being at their mercy, especially during the early part of the day when he sun was in the eastern sky. Even from Hornchurch or Gravesend, we found that flying to the Channel at our maximum climbing speed we often arrived below the fighters, which were waiting above to pounce (to 'jump', or 'bounce') us.

DOG-FIGHT WITH ME 109S

We did three trips on 28 July 1940. The first two were uneventful, but the last one, at 15.00 hours, was for a convoy near Dover. Messerschmitt Bf 109Es of *Jagdgeschwader* 51, led by the veteran *Geschwaderkommodore Major* Werner Mölders, clashed with our Spitfires of 41 Squadron. It was a fighter skirmish which was in many ways typical of those of the Battle of Britain. *Major* Werner Mölders was leading a force comprising the I and II/JG 51 with orders to escort bombers on a convoy raid.

The squadron was ordered to scramble at 2.30 p.m., thirty minutes after the first indications of an enemy raid headed for Dover. It was to reinforce one Spitfire squadron and two Hurricane squadrons, which had previously been directed against the enemy aircraft. Our squadron comprised three Spitfires in Blue Section led by Sqn Ldr Hood, three in Yellow Section led by Plt Off Bennions, three more in Red Section and two in Green Section led by Flt Lt Webster and myself as Green 3.

Green 2 was positioned 1,000 feet below the main formation, keeping an eye out for possible attacks from below. Arriving over Dover, 41 Squadron began a circling climb up to its assigned patrol altitude of 20,000 feet. As the eleven Spitfires approached the coast in a climbing turn, we were attacked from above by the German aircraft. Two Bf 109Es flown by Gebhardt and Mölders penetrated the formation. The Bf 109Es had the advantage of greater height, but on this occasion they did not achieve complete tactical surprise. A warning was called by Webster in Green 1, and the Spitfires broke away from the attack.

Sqn Ldr H.R.L. 'Robin' Hood; leading his squadron as Blue 1, broke away to port, followed by his wingman, Flg Off A.D.J. 'Lulu' Lovell (Blue 2). *Gefreiter* Gebhardt chased Hood, closely followed by Plt Off Bennions, who used his boost to catch the German. Despite this evasive manoeuvre, Mölders was able to pull in behind Lovell's Spitfire and open fire. Flt Lt J.T. Webster, flying as Green 1, had spotted the Bf 109Es coming in to the attack, and warned the rest of the formation. He then ordered me to form line astern, from the vic formation in which we had been flying.

Webster gave chase to Mölders's Bf 109E and opened fire on it, shortly after Mölders had begun his attack on Blue 2. I supported my leader by firing at Mölders from a quarter position. I followed closer to a hundred yards and saw this fire take effect, and the Bf 109E executed a half-roll and dived away. Mölders was wounded in the leg, and he pulled up in a vertical climb to evade the Spitfires. This succeeded but then an uncontrolled spin occurred. Recovery out of the spin was achieved and Mölders nursed his damaged fighter back to the French coast, where he crash-landed at Wissant. 'Lulu' Lovell was also wounded, and brought his Spitfire down and crash-landed on Manston airfield. 'Lulu' was lucky, as his cockpit was awash with fuel. At the same time as Webster made his attack, Plt Off G.H. Bennions (Yellow 1) had caught up with and shot down a second Bf 109E, piloted by *Gefreiter* Gebhardt, which was pursuing Blue 1's Spitfire. Further Bf 109Es dived into the combat and Webster (Green 1) chased one of them out to sea. He was able to fire several short bursts before he spotted further Bf 109Es closing in behind. He then broke off the combat and flew back to the English coast at wave-top height. (See Appendix 14.)

Surviving a dog fight was not the only hurdle to overcome: getting home and landing in one piece was the next task. After this skirmish Webster's damaged aircraft crash-landed at base but he was unhurt. Bennions's Spitfire was badly damaged after taking some enemy fire too and landed his wreck perfectly at Manston airfield with his wheels down and no flaps. Scott was

Sgt E A 'Shippy' Shipman at Catterick, 25th July 1938. *[RAF Crown Copyright]*

RAF Uxbridge – recruitment training. Squad in full marching order for 24 hour guard duty. Sgt Andrews (ex Scots Guards) on far left. Front rank No.2 'Jock' Hamilton, No.3 Jim Berry, No.4 E A Shipman, Rear rank No.8 'Dizzy Baker. *[E A Shipman]*

Vickers Virginia
Night Bomber 1931.
Powered by two
Napier Lion engines.
My first night flight
as a passenger was in
the rear gunner's
cockpit – obscured by
the upper tail plane.
A lonely place.
[E A Shipman]

Armstrong Whitworth Atlas. Powered by Armstrong Siddeley Jaguar radial engine. No 16 Army Cooperation Squadron RAF Old Sarum 1931. *[E A Shipman]*

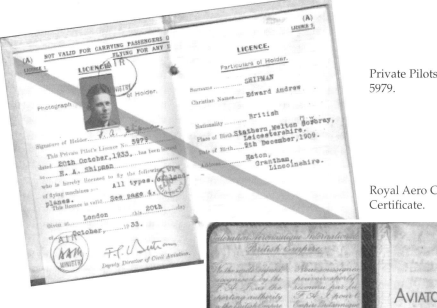

Private Pilots licence No. 5979.

Royal Aero Club Aviator's Certificate.

Ab initio trainee pilots at Brough February 1936. Taking a break for a photo in between flying B2's. Back row: Appleton, Roman, Le Voi, Shipman, Kime, Smith. Front row: Campbell, Benson, Gasgoine, Robertson, Boxhall. "Pongo" Scarf was not present – he later was awarded the VC in WW II.

Results of Gasgoine's 'prang' at night in an Audax. *[EA Shipman]*

Result of a solo flight on windy day. *[E A Shipman]*

Another windy day and a solo flight ends in a bent aeroplane. *[E A Shipman]*

E A 'Shippy' Shipman (left) in full flying gear ready for open cockpit flying. Sgt Eddie Womphey instructor (below) E A Shipman (below left) at Practice Camp at North Coates.

"Shippy" Shipman piloting Hawker Demon of B Flight, 41 Squadron in a battle climb during 1937. 172 hours on this type. *[E A Shipman]*

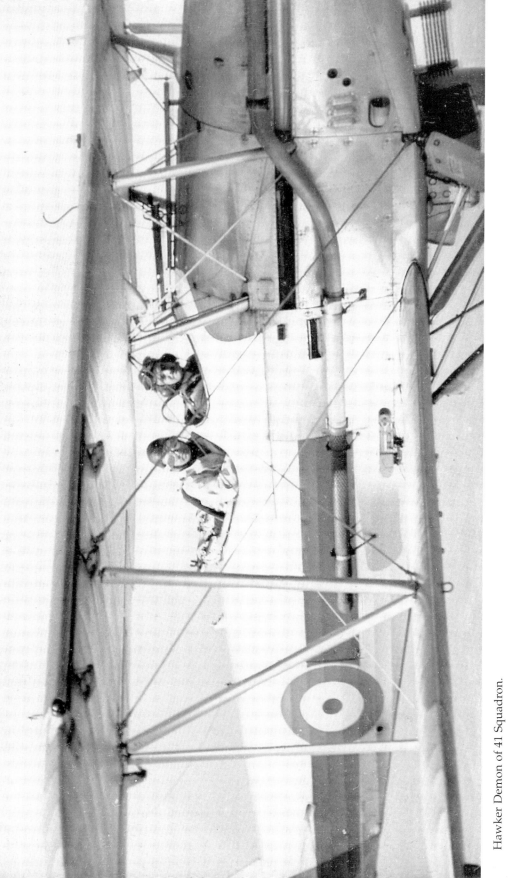

Hawker Demon of 41 Squadron.

Top left: Hawker Furies II, Above: Hawker Demons B Flight, Left: Hawker Furies II, Bottom right: Hawker Fury II 41 Squadron RAF Catterick 1937-38. [E A Shipman]

Hawker Fury Mk I of 41 Squadron, 1938. *[E A Shipman]*

41 Squadron badge worn on flying overalls. The cross of St Omer was presented to 41 Squadron in France 1914-18.

Precision flying by pilots of 41 Squadron in Hawker Fury Mk II Numbers from the top – down: K7280; K7268; K7274; K7269; K7263; K7271; K7265; K7279; K7270. Log book shows that "Shippy" flew the following aircraft together with several others in the Squadron: K7268; K7269; K7263; K7271; K7265; K7270. The worst position to fly was as No. 9 for in echelon one was flying at the end of a long line of nine or more aircraft which tended to whiplash if the station keeping was not steady. Bumpy conditions, of course, made the situation worse and at the end of a flight one's arms and legs ached like mad.

Ministry of Defence – Royal Air force News Crown Copyright]

After the wedding at 49 Brook
Terrace, Darlington, 17th
August 1938.

Some members of 41 Squadron in 1938
(from left to right) Bennions, Blatchford,
Ryder, Sayers and Harris. Probably with
Wallace behind the camera *[Eleanor
Collins (formerly Harris)]*

Spitfire of B Flight 41 Squadron after the wooden, fixed pitch two bladed propellers were replaced with two position pitch types with three blades of a slightly shorter length. *[E A Shipman]*

Spitfire Mk I of 41 Squadron. *[E A Shipman]*

"Shippy" Shipman running up 'EBL' a three bladed Spitfire Mk I Number N3126.

Spitfire Mk I of 41 Squadron
[E A Shipman]

"Wally" Wallens

Albert "Bill" Harris on left and "Shippy" Shipman.
[E A Shipman]

Pilot Officer the Lord Guisborough,
Intelligence Officer 41 Squadron, Master of
Fox Hounds of the Cleveland Hunt and an ex
Prisoner of War of WWI. *[Steve Brew]*

Members of 41 Squadron relaxing. From left to right: Sgt Harris (killed in a Whitley accident), Sayers,
Sgt "Shippy" Shipman, Flying Officer Norman Ryder and Pilot Officer "Pooky" Overall (killed whilst
night flying).

Some of the pilots of 41 Squadron April 1940 Back row from left to right: "Mitzi" Darling, Ford, Sayers Howitt, Carr-Lewty. Middle row from left to right: Copley, Durrant, MacKenzie, unknown, Cory, Lovell, Stapleton, Wallens, Front row from left to right: Unknown, Legard, Wng Cdr Carter, Sqdn Ldr Hood, Ryder, Stevens, Gamblen. *[Steve Brew]*

Sqdn Ldr Hilary Richard Lionel "Robin" Hood DFC. CO of No 41 Squadron. Killed 5.9.40. Age 32.

unhurt as he landed his damaged Spitfire, wheels up at Manston. MacKenzie, too, crash-landed, unhurt, but wheels up in a field.

The next morning, 29 July 1940, we went to Manston at dawn. It was a fine and cloudless day, and eleven of us were ordered off to defend a convoy off Dover against some forty-eight Ju 87s. When we found them they were bombing Dover harbour, and while we were going after them about eight Me 109s came down out of the sun. 'A' Flight took on the 109s while we continued to chase the Ju 87s. A bad day for us, for in the first clash a 109 sent Flg Off D.R. Gamblen ('B') down to crash vertically into the sea just outside the harbour (this was the first time I had seen one of our chaps go down and hit the surface). Then another 109 put the 'B' Flight Commander, Flt Lt Webster, out of action. He managed to crash-land unhurt at Manston. Later we found that 'A' Flight had three others crash-land at Manston. All we could claim were two 109s damaged and five Ju 87s destroyed.

This episode shows the penalty of not knowing the presence of 109s above, and of arriving at the scene so far below the escorting fighters, which we could not see against the bright sun. Later that day we did one more shipping patrol, with what aircraft we had left, but there was no opposition this time.

During the next four days I went on seven shipping patrols, usually as Green Leader, However, on none of these sorties did we see any opposition. Then on 5 August 1940 we patrolled the Dover area again to cover a convoy. On this occasion I was Blue 2 behind the CO, Sqn Ldr 'Robin' Hood. This time we had arranged Green Section to act as 'rear-end Charlie'. The job of this section was to fly behind and above us, weaving from side to side so as to keep a look-out against fighters coming down on us from behind and out of the sun. RT was used as little as possible so that a warning call might not be missed.

The weather on this occasion was perfect, not a cloud in the sky, and the visibility so good that at a height of well over 20,000 feet we could see the French coast in great detail and well into France. For once, we felt reasonably confident that we were in a position to do justice to our task if the convoy far below was attacked, and because of our look-out section we felt safer than was usual.

After some time we were warned of a build-up of activity over the French airfields, and our concentration was for any signs of bombers coming out. We had not long to wait before we spotted a formation of aircraft circling the French coast, and this appeared to be of squadron strength. Almost immediately we saw another formation, and another. They appeared to be joining up into a large formation, and soon looked like a swarm of bees. They continued circling and climbing, and then, although still below our height, seemed to be starting to cross the Channel. Without doubt they were fighters and not bombers, but we thought they might be the escorting fighters for bombers coming in behind.

The CO made a quick RT call to our look-out section, but there was no reply, so he asked me to look for them – they were nowhere to be seen! As I was reporting this, the leader of Green Section himself reported that he was just landing his section at Manston to rearm and refuel! Apparently he had gone after some aircraft he had seen, and much to the CO's annoyance and the detriment of our safety, had left us unprotected without a word of warning. His efforts were in vain, as he failed to get anything.

In the meantime, the 'swarm of bees' was still climbing and getting nearer and nearer. In keeping our ground controller informed of the events, the CO, when asked how many aircraft there were, replied in his typical way, 'It looks like the whole bloody *Luftwaffe*, old boy!' Then, just as we were contemplating our problem of three aircraft against this large formation, they turned round and went back to France! What a fortuitous turn of events, under the circumstances.

'THE BENDS'

The pot started coming to the boil on 8 August 1940, as German fighters swept across the Channel. *JGs* 3, 26, 51, 53 and 54 were engaged by our Spitfires. The German aircraft were targeting the convoy Peewit, which consisted of twenty-nine vessels, including Royal Navy escorts and their own balloon barrage. On this sortie, which lasted one hour and forty minutes, I had been experiencing aching pains in my arms, and more particularly in my elbows. On 8 August we again patrolled Dover, but this time at 28,000 feet. As well as 41 Squadron, 64, 65 and 610 were involved. Throughout the one hour and thirty minutes of this trip, the pains in my elbows and shoulders were severe, and my knees hurt, too. I was suffering from 'the bends'. At the time I did not know what the trouble was and actually wondered if I would be able to control my aeroplane properly because the arm joints were so painful. Fortunately the condition did not get any worse and I managed to last out the trip. I was very relieved to get to a lower altitude where the air pressure was greater and more normal.

Our flight, 'B', had no part in the combat which 'A' Flight was doing on this trip – they claimed two Me 109s damaged. Diving from 25,000 to 12,000 feet, 'Wally' Wallens and Terry attacked one Me 109 from astern. This crashed into the sea. In the mêlée that followed 'Wally' picked another one off, and it too dived steeply into the sea. Returning to Manston, 'Wally' rearmed and refuelled, and immediately took off, climbing to 12,000 feet. As he did so he intercepted a lone Me 109 returning home. Following a short burst from a very close fifty yards, the Me 109 also crashed into the sea.

Honours on this day were roughly even, with four Spitfires being shot down and three pilots killed. A fifth Spitfire force-landed and a further two were damaged. A Blenheim of 600 Squadron was also lost. German losses were a single Me 109 shot down, four more that crash-landed in France and a sixth badly damaged.[8] Later in the afternoon we returned to Catterick after we had been relieved by 54 Squadron.

AN INNOVATION

During the early days of the Battle of Britain the glaring need for eyes in the back of one's head became so obvious. At best it was difficult to turn the head round sufficiently to see anything coming in from behind, and the need for a constant rearward look-out to avoid being 'jumped' upon put a great physical strain on the neck and eyes. The Technical Officer at Hornchurch had a brainwave – he jumped in his car and bought up all the car rear-view mirrors he could find, and fitted them to the aircraft. At first they were fixed centrally and just inside the top of the wind-screen; but then to improve the visibility they were repositioned outside the windscreen but still at the top. Eventually they became essential basic equipment for fighters.

THE AIR FIGHTING SCENE

When two opposing fighter formations meet in battle there is usually a rapid and remarkable change of scene. The attackers break up their large formation into smaller and more manoeuvrable units and dive down at their selected targets, preferably from above and from out of the sun. The target formation breaks up immediately the attack becomes obvious, and the smaller units form a circling protective pattern. As the attackers single out their individual targets, by this time no doubt one against one, it is a case of trying to out-turn one another in order for the attacker to get his gunsights on the target or for the target to evade successfully.

Of course the primary aim of the attacker is to achieve complete surprise from a quick attack from up sun and from a greater altitude. These tactics, if successful, will inevitably split up the formation, and then it is usually every man for himself unless there are specific orders, say, to go after bombers or fighter escorts.

The most amazing thing about this form of attack and the dog-fighting which usually follows is that, certainly to the pilots involved, one moment the sky is full of aeroplanes, and within seconds – it's empty! Seldom can you get together again as a section, much less as a flight, to return home in an orderly fashion, and it is usually a case of trying to find another target – that is if you are not one yourself – and finally going home alone.

NOTES

1. In early 1940, radio communications from British aircraft involved the use of TR9D HF transmitter-receivers. These units generally gave poor performance and were vulnerable to interference. Each squadron operated at a different frequency, which made communications with sector stations and other squadrons difficult, particularly when operating some distance from the sector station. The use of later VHF sets greatly improved matters, in both quality and range of reception/transmission. However, while these were available at the time of the Dunkirk evacuation, the VHF sets were replaced with old TR9D units for fear that one might fall into enemy hands for evaluation.
2. Richard Townshend Bickers, *The Battle of Britain*.
3. Story courtesy of 'Wally' Wallens.
4. Patrick Bishop, *Fighter Boys*.
5. Gerald Langley, killed in action 15 September 1940.
6. Eric Lock, killed in action 3 August 1941.
7. Shot down twenty-two German aircraft and one shared.
8. Richard Townshend Bickers, *The Battle of Britain*.

CHAPTER 9

Back at Catterick

For the next few days it was forward readiness at the Greatham base and a scramble on most days.

It was on 11 August 1940 that Green Section of 41 Squadron was called into action. A Ju 88A-1 (7A + KH) of 1/*Aufklarungsgrupppe* 121 based at Stavanger, Norway, was ordered to carry out a high-altitude photo-reconnaissance mission of the Bomber Command aerodromes at Dishforth and Linton-on-Ouse. At 6.25 p.m. radar identified the raiders, and three Spitfires of Green Section, 'B' Flight, 41 Squadron, were ordered off from Catterick to patrol Teesmouth and be ready for an interception. Flg Off John Boyle (Green 2) spotted the Junkers at 18,000 feet and chased the German aircraft. A quick burst from the Spitfire at a range of 500 yards brought return fire from the dorsal gun of the Junkers. John Boyle broke away at a distance of a hundred yards, and 'Wally' Wallens (Green 1) took up the chase just as both aircraft entered cloud. 'Wally' fired at a range of forty yards, which reduced further to twenty-five yards in the cloud. 'Wally' was able to identify the position of the target, and continued firing using the sparks from his tracer bullets as they struck the Junkers in the zero visibility. 'Wally' disabled the Junkers's port engine. Sgt 'Mitzi' Darling (Green 3) had hung back and eventually spotted the Junkers above the cloud base. An attack from quarter to astern used all the Spitfire's ammunition. The Junkers descended slowly for a forced landing on Newton Moor. The Royal Observer Corps plot record for 11 August 1940 (15.54 and 19.45 hours) showed tracks of the Ju 88 A-1 (7A + KH) over Whitby at the first sighting, and then the Spitfires of 41 Squadron were observed intercepting the Ju 88 over Redcar.

The Greatest Day

Further action took place on 15 August 1940. This later became known as 'The Greatest Day'. There was activity all around the English coast as the *Luftwaffe* flew over two thousand sorties – more than any other single day in the Battle of Britain.[1]

At 12.38 hours the whole squadron was ordered off from Catterick to patrol Hartlepool at 15,000 feet, and to intercept a large raid approaching the Newcastle area from the north-east. The weather was extensively cloudy, and this was the first time the German High Command had sent out simultaneously all three air fleets – *Luftflotte* 2 from Holland, Belgium and northern France, *Luftflotte* 3 from north and west France, and *Luftflotte* 5 from Norway and Denmark. Fifty bombers of *KG* 30 had been briefed to strike at Driffield aerodrome. Sixty-three Heinkel 111s of *KG* 26 had Dishforth and Linton-on-Ouse aerodromes as their primary targets, with Newcastle, Sunderland and Middlesbrough as their secondary aiming points. A naval convoy, codename Arena, had left Hull at mid-day, and there was significant radar vigilance because of this.

Two *Staffeln* of Heinkel seaplanes flew towards Dundee as a feint to lure the fighters northwards. The main raid consisted of seventy-two He 111s of *KG* 26. Due to a navigation error or a mis-reading of the wind direction and speed, the main raid approached the coast nearer Edinburgh than the planned landfall. A correction to the south consumed more fuel, and finally they met up with their escort of twenty-one long-range Bf 110Ds of *I/ZG* 76.

The Heinkels, with their lion badge and motto *'Vestigium Leonis'* on the fuselage, carried 3,000 pounds of bombs (incendiaries, 500 kg and 250 kg high explosives) and were escorted by twenty-one Messerschmitt 110 twin-engined fighter planes of *I/ZG* 76.

Our squadron of thirteen aircraft was to back up 72 Squadron, which had gone off from Acklington with eleven Spitfires, and six Hurricanes of 605 Squadron from Drem. There were also to follow twelve Hurricanes of 79 Squadron from Acklington. Off the Farne Islands, No. 72 Squadron attacked the incoming He 111s, which were without their deadly escorts at this time. They scattered the formation, which jettisoned its bombs and obtained three confirmed kills, although they claimed several more.

No. 41 Squadron was led by Norman Ryder, but over Hartlepool the command was passed to Plt Off George 'Ben' Bennions, as Norman's radio was unserviceable. Ground control advised the squadron of an interception heading '100 bandits[2] on Vector 010'. The thirteen Spitfires of 41 Squadron sped northwards over the sea. The cloud ceiling was at 5,000 feet, with some breaks and haze above that reduced visibility to about five miles.

The six aircraft of Blue and Green Sections were ordered to attack the fighter escort while 'Ben' Bennions deployed the seven aircraft of Red and Yellow Sections into echelon starboard formation for a beam attack on the bombers.

Climbing up to 18,000 feet through and above the cloud, in my Mark I Spitfire K9805, one could hear much activity on the RT. I was leading Green Section with Plt Off G. Langley and Sgt Usmar, and the raid was reported as thirty plus. In fact there were sixty-three Heinkel 111s escorted by twenty-one Me 110 twin-engined fighters.

In no time the vastly outnumbered Spitfires were among the raiders and their escorts. The mêlée had begun and all hell had broken loose.

GREEN SECTION TAKES ON THE INVADERS

The weather on 15 August was fine, but there was a fair amount of cloud between about 10,000 and 15,000 feet. It was almost full cover inland of Newcastle. I was scrambled to 18,000 feet over Durham at 13.00 hours – the raid was reported as thirty-plus at first, but this was later increased to 170 Me 110s and He 111s.

I was ordered to engage the Me 110s which were escorting the bombers. Turning in behind a flight of Messerschmitts on the left of the formation, I ordered my chaps to form echelon port to do a 'Number Three' attack (which really meant three against three line astern). Before getting into firing range, the targets turned hard to port and came straight for us. I doubt if they had seen us, for the Me 110s didn't appear to fire at us, which they could have done with their four machine-guns and two cannon in the nose. This was most unexpected, and our training did not prepare us for this tactic. They weren't supposed to do this! Our previous battle training was about one hour per day at most and had been based on formation flying with a flight of three aircraft. I fired at the first Messerschmitt head on from about 400 yards with a short burst of two seconds' duration. This was a bit risky because of the very fast closing speed, probably in excess of 600 mph. There was little time for a steady and considered aim but it seemed a chance not to be missed. One moment the windscreen was full of enemy aircraft approaching at an alarming speed, and then a second later the sky appeared empty as the Me 110 disappeared behind me. There was no return of fire, and the result could not be seen and no claim was made, but I could have been successful in at least damaging the 110. The Me 110 broke away at very close range to my left and disappeared.

Picking up another Me 110, which evaded violently in steep turns to the left with some climbing followed by some diving, I then attacked the aircraft from astern at a range of about 200 yards. This was a prolonged engagement which used up the remainder of my ammunition. The starboard engine of the Me 110 belched clouds of smoke and appeared to be on fire. I believe I had put it out of action. Then the aircraft made an erratic turn to port and disappeared into the cloud below, apparently out of control. I claimed this as damaged and a probable. It was subsequently confirmed as a kill from the camera-gun film assessment and the record of an Me 110 crashing about three miles east of Barnard Castle. This was the only occasion when the camera gun actually worked. In this engagement our squadron got seven confirmed and several probables at the expense of one bullet hole! Sgt Usmar in my section also got an Me 110.

The Me 110, serial number 3155, carrying the marking M8 + CH, and piloted by *Oberleutnant* Hans Ulrich Kettling, that crash-landed near Barnard Castle was officially recorded as being shot down by myself and Plt Off 'Ben' Bennions [See the transcript of my combat report, and also the transcript from the Air Fighting Development Unit (AFDU) report].

In 1987, forty-seven years after the encounter with the Me 110, I was to meet the pilot, Hans Kettling, once again, and help him to find the field where the crash-landing took place. We swapped stories and mementoes and remained good friends after our second meeting.

I recalled the details. My colleague, Plt Off 'Ben' Bennions (Yellow 1), was positioning himself behind the Heinkels when an Me 110 slid onto his tail. Evasive manoeuvres or 'jinking' to port

---

Transcript from Air Fighting Development Unit (AFDU) report

AFDU 29/8/40
Ref: AFDU/19/13
Film No. 99
P/O E.A. Shipman, No. 41 Squadron
Date: 15/8/40
Me 110

Overlapping frames have spoilt this film for assessment purposes. The first 8½ seconds worth contains nothing and may have been shot on the ground. There follows a burst of 2½, 1, 3½, and 22 seconds respectively. The first apparently a head-on attack, as the speed of closing from 650 yards to 190 yards is approximately 400 mph.

The second shows a full beam attack from about 400 yards and a third astern at 250 yards. The last very long burst is of astern attack with the EA continuously climbing and flattening out. Corrections are being made and aim is steady and appears to be very good.

The EA's starboard engine is on fire towards the end.

(signed) B.W.N. Mullen for W/Cdr, AFDU

Catt/S33/10/air (Probable)

---

and starboard got him out of the firing line and behind another Me 110 at 300 yards' range. A three-second burst from 'Ben's' Spitfire resulted in the De Wilde tracer shells striking the Me 110's fuselage. There was no reply from the rear gunner. The recoil from the guns had slowed the Spitfire down so that 'Ben' was now about 400 yards astern of the Me 110. The Me 110 immediately dived for cloud cover on a south-westerly course. 'Ben' dived after the German pilot, closing very slowly. He was travelling very fast indeed and getting closer to the clouds. 'Ben' gave him another three-second burst before entering the clouds. When 'Ben' came out of the clouds, he found himself midway between Piercebridge

and Barnard Castle – about fifty miles from the point of interception. He reported to control that he thought he had just shot
down an Me 110 in this area but didn't see him actually land or
crash.

Flg Off Tony 'Lulu' Lovell (Blue 1) chose the last of a line of
three Me 110s. A concentrated burst of fire caused his target to
explode. His second target succumbed to an eleven-second burst,
and this fell away out of control. Sgt Howitt (Blue 2) raked the
third Me 110 from nose to tail, and it too plunged earth-bound,
trailing smoke towards the clouds 13,000 feet below. Plt Off
'Wally' Wallens (Green 3) avoided a head-on collision with an
Me 110 with a half-roll that brought another into his sights. A burst
from the .303 Brownings sent the Me 110 smoking into the clouds.
Sgt Usmar (Green 3) saw an Me 110 crossing to attack 'Wally'. As
the Me 110 passed in front at very close range – 50 yards – a short
burst was fired. The result was not observed as a Heinkel bomber
was now on a collision course with Sgt Usmar, and a further burst
resulted in the Heinkel exploding at short range with such force
that Sgt Usmar's Spitfire was thrown upwards about forty feet.

Yellow and Red Sections were tackling the Heinkel bombers.
After the first beam attack the two Spitfire sections went under the
bomber group and then climbed behind them. Norman Ryder
(Yellow 2) went in to attack line astern of the bombers, but he was
fired upon by an Me 110. He evaded and executed a tight 360-
degree turn to get behind his attacker. Three bursts of fire from
the Spitfire resulted in pieces of Me 110 fuselage flying off, and
then a large explosion – the central fuel tank. Flg Off John
MacKenzie (Red 1) had selected an Me 110 just starboard of the
main formation. At 200 yards he opened fire and the Me 110's
starboard engine smoked as the raider dived for cloud cover.

My log-book entry reads very factually as follows:

Date and hour	Aeroplane type and No.	Pilot	Time	Duty
Aug 15 12:38	Spitfire I EB L	Self	1:00	Patrol Seaham 20,000 ft. G 1, Flight 6 E/A, Self 1 Me 110

Transcript from P/O Shipman's combat report for 15 August 1940

Combat Report
Date: 15/8/40
Squadron: No. 41 Spitfires
Section: Green
Time: 13.00 hrs
Place: Durham vicinity and the west
Aircraft: Reported 30 + but were about 60 various, mostly Me 110s

Leading Green Section I was ordered to attack the fighter escort of Me 110s and at 18000ft I ordered my section 'echelon port' to carry out a No. 3 attack on a section of Me 110s on the left of the formation.

Before getting into range, the E.A. turned left about quickly and headed straight for me. I engaged the first one with a head on attack at about 400yrds range firing a short burst of about 2 seconds. The E.A. broke away to my port at a very close range. No return fire was noticed and no result was seen. The E. A. disappeared behind me.

I then engaged another Me110 with a series of deflection shots at various ranges, the E.A. evading violently. No effect was seen and no return fire was experienced.

The same E.A. was then attacked from the astern position at about 200 yards range. I fired the rest of my ammunition with the result that the starboard engine was put out of action with clouds of smoke. The E.A. then made erratic turn to the left and disappeared into cloud below, apparently out of control.

(signed) E.A. Shipman P/O

REPORT FROM NORWAY[3]

At the airfield of Stavanger-Sola in Norway, 11.00 hrs (German time), 15 August, the Heinkels of III *Gruppe/Kempf-geschwader* 26 (III/KG 26) took off for the mission to England. *Gruppen Kommandeur Major* Gunther Wolfien led the aircraft

across the North Sea on a long flight to bomb Dishforth.
All the crews had been briefed that only a token force of
RAF fighters would meet them, and they would be taken care
of by their fighter escort – a fatal error for many flying this
day.

The lead *Kette* of 8 *Staffel/KG* 26⁴ was headed by its *Staffel
Kapitan, Hauptmann* Stephan; to his left flew *Oberleutnant*
Horst von Besser, to his right flew an experienced pilot
Oberleutnant Hermann Riedel. III/*KG* 26 soon formatted
on the aircraft of its *Gruppen Kommandeur* and then joined
elements of the *Geschwader*. Initially, close escort was provided by Messerschmitt 110s of 1/*Jagdgeschwader* 77, but
when their maximum range was reached the close escort was
handed over to the Messerschmitt 110s of *Zerstorergeschwader*
76, led by *Hauptmann* Werner Restemeyer. The flight of this
massive formation was uneventful, but about sixty miles
from the English coast a series of warnings came over the
radio and all crews became noticeably nervous, anxiously
scanning the skies for the enemy. Hermann Riedel spotted
several fighters converging in a wide curve, which then
dived through the fighters, heading for the bombers. This
was 72 Squadron, whose Spitfires shot down *Hauptmann*
Restemeyer and probably *Oberleutnant* Gustav Loobes.
Surprisingly the bombers of III/*KG* 26 continued unscathed,
soon crossing the coast and continuing west (the pre-flight
briefing said they were to turn south).

The Messerschmitt 110s of *Zerstorergeschwader* 76 joined the
bomber formation at the English coast. Each aircraft was fitted
with a special long-range, belly-mounted fuel tank called a
Dackelbauch, or 'dachshund-belly tank', and two discardable
wing drop-tanks. Hans Kettling in M8+C remembered that
the formation looked impressive in the clear summer sunshine, and he could see for miles, despite the slight haze.
During the attack from 72 Squadron the Me 110s of Loobes
and Restemeyer exploded due to hits in their belly tanks.
Hans Kettling continued until he heard his radio operator
opening fire. Hans Kettling looked in his mirror to see three
Spitfires in pursuit. This was Green Section of 41 Squadron
led by P/O Ted Shipman.

Oberleutnant Hans Ulrich Kettling, pilot of 1/ZG 76, recalls his version of the encounter:[5]

Our orders on 15 August were to leave Stavanger in Norway in our Me Bf 110s[6] and protect the He 111s of *KG* 26 which would attack airbases in northern England. Since our Me 110s could not reach England and return with standard fuel tanks, we had one additional fuel tank under the belly and one under each wing. The idea was to use the fuel in the wing tanks first, then to discard them over the sea and to reach England with the belly tank as the sole handicap. This ungainly blister was a handicap enough – it made the plane several kilometres per hour slower, and the unused fuel sloshed around, making steering and aiming unstable, and since the tank was made from plywood, it was highly flammable. We were all anything but happy to perform our first long-range raid with our mutilated planes.

The weather was fair and sunny with a slight haze over the sea – a very typical August day. We were told that special precautions had been taken to avoid premature detection, but at about twenty miles from the English coast, the first of several waves of Spitfires came in for a fight.

Our altitude was about 15,000 feet, and our formation dis-integrated into *Schwarm*,[7] attacking the Spitfires and keeping them away from the bombers, which had to continue on their course. All around dog-fights developed rapidly, and I followed my Number One, *Oblt* Helmut Lent [later to become a highly successful and decorated night-fighter pilot], who went after two Spits to protect his rear. I heard *Ogefr.* Volk working his machine-gun, and looking back, I stared into the flaming machine-guns of four Spitfires in splendid formation. They were coming straight towards me.

My plane was hit, not severely, but the right engine went dead, lost coolant and the oil temperature rose rapidly. I had to switch off the engine and feather the propeller and tried to reach the protection of the bombers, which were overhead in close formation. I was not successful – the plane was slow and I could not gain height. Over the radio, I heard the boys in the bombers talking about my plane, so I gave my 'Mayday' because the Spits came in for the second attack and the kill . . . . This time they got the left engine of my Me 110, my *Bordfunker* (radio operator) and the front windscreen (the tracer bullets missing me by a fraction of inches). *Ogefr.* Volk was lying on the floor, covered with blood and unconscious. I had no means of ascertaining whether he was alive or not.

Since all flight controls were in perfect order (without the engines, of course) and the belly tank empty, I decided to bring the Me 110 down for a belly landing. I dived away from the fighting, down and down, leaving the lethal Spitfires behind and looking for a suitable landing site. I eased the plane carefully down over a very large meadow, but on touching down, I found the speed was still rather high. Finally, it crashed through a low stone wall which was hidden by a hedge, leaving the rear fuselage behind which broke just behind the cockpit. Looking back I saw the rubber dinghy, which was stowed in a partition under the fuselage and fixed with a long cable to the side of the cockpit, dangling behind along the meadow, inflating itself and following like a dog – a very grotesque sight. The plane came to a halt at last. I jumped out, freed Volk and carried him to a safe distance, fearing fire and explosion. I disabled the radio with some shots from my pistol and I tried to set the plane on fire, but the two incendiaries we carried for this purpose did not work as expected. One of them burned my right hand badly, and that was the only honourable wound I had in the whole adventure. After that, a lot of people (heaven knows where they all came from) came running armed with sticks and stones, threatening and shouting from a distance until some red-capped Military Police took over and transported Volk, who had in some way recovered, and me to the police station of a nearby village, where we were locked in two cells.

A doctor came and took care of Volk, who was after all not so very badly wounded, and he took care of my burnt hand, too. We got an excellent dinner, with the compliments and good wishes from the local military big-shot. Several RAF officers came and asked questions, and I think one of them was the pilot who shot me down. I went through these hours as in a trance – I only wanted to sleep. . . . In the night two soldiers escorted me to London by train. Mr Volk went to hospital. We arrived in the grey hours of the morning and drove through the bomb-littered streets. The soldiers delivered me at Cockfosters, which as it turned out was an interrogation centre. The fighting part of war was over for me. For the rest of the war I was a prisoner in both Wales and Canada, before returning to Mettman in Germany.

[See the further account in Appendix 9, where Hans recollects his post-crash memories in a letter dated January 1980. See also the eyewitness accounts from the ground in Appendix 10.]

In 1980 Hans Kettling came to visit me and we swapped stories, pictures and some mementoes. In 1987 he came to stay with me again, and we journeyed to his crash-landing site. I investigated the possible site of the crash-landing, and after consulting several sources discovered it was at Broomielaw Farm. I had made enquiries with Durham Police and they kindly agreed to meet us at Broomielaw Farm, three miles east of Barnard Castle (OS Map Ref. 088179), with the owner's daughter, Mrs Phillips.

NOTES

1. 15 August became known by the *Luftwaffe* as 'Black Thursday'. The RAF lost thirty-four aircraft (two on the ground), and the *Luftwaffe* seventy-five.
2. Enemy Aircraft. German equivalent *Feindliche Jäger/Autos*.
3. Chris Goss, *Black Thursday*.
4. The *Luftwaffe* equivalent of the squadron was the *Staffel*, also consisting of approximately twelve aircraft.
5. Chris Goss, *The* Luftwaffe *Fighters' Battle of Britain*.
6. Bf 110D-1/R-1 Wk Nr 3155 M8+CH.
7. *Schwarm* – a small group, usually of four aircraft.

CHAPTER 10

Interviews in 1990

Later in 1990 Hans and I were both invited to stay in a London hotel and be interviewed and photographed for a large feature in the July edition of the *The Times Saturday Review*. Several meetings with Hans in the UK and Germany brought us closer together, and my friendship with him after the conflict was probably stronger than with some of the RAF pilots. I lost many colleagues and friends during the war, and, of course, for those who did survive there were individual career paths that diverged quickly and in many directions.

During the interviews for the newspaper there were many searching questions, particularly about our feelings and thoughts during the conflict in the air. These were answered by myself and by Hans with honesty. I had never sought to put them down or to try and convince other people that my feelings were the right ones or that they were even important. However, with the interviews the questions were asked and duly answered.[1]

Hans has sharp memories of the encounter when Ted's Spitfire 'poured a packet' at him:

> I cannot tell you my feelings. Not because I have forgotten, but because almost certainly I felt nothing. Maybe for one half-second it was, 'Hell, they have me', but all my concentration was on staying alive. People who have been in air combat and tell you they thought this or they felt that are liars. At such times you function like a robot. Fear? Not even that. Never once in crucial moments in air fighting did I have fear. Anger? Yes. But this is also odd, never anger at the

British enemy, but at the orders that had put me there, or the lack of support. When Shipman got me, only after I was put in a cell did I react. I fell back and slept for three hours.

He recalled his earlier days:

I had wanted to be a sailor. In the 1930s vacancies in the German merchant fleets were scarce. Then in 1936 my headmaster called the class together and said the new *Luftwaffe* was seeking bright young men. I was desperately interested. I had been fascinated by First World War pilots landing their wartime planes in farm fields. So a chance to fly! As a career or as an expression of patriotism? As a career absolutely. Things were hard in Germany then. But I do not back away from what you ask. I was in the Nazi Youth. Not an ardent Nazi, but a patriotic German, yes.

I opted for fighter command. Why? The speed. The aerobatics. Because you would be alone, dependent on no one, and, yes, the glamour. I joined the wing that bore the name of Richthofen. Can you imagine that for a young man's pride?

Hans Kettling's *Staffel* had been preparing for war. Older pilots who had flown the older Me 109 in Spain praised this machine:

It did not feel like going to war as we annexed Austria, nor later when troops marched into Czechoslovakia. We were told we were going into these countries to protect our borders from foreign intrigue by France and Russia. Maybe to say that we believed that seems stupid. But we did. Perhaps we wanted to believe. Perhaps we were young. Also because we were so uninterested. Politics, pah! Anyway we had these 109s. I was very proud. Some weapon. There was a bit of resistance in Czechoslovakia. They had a few biplanes, but we got most of them on the ground. War, it seemed then, was very easy.

Before the onslaught of Poland, Hans's *Staffel* was re-equipped with Me 110s:

Not a fighter, a destroyer. With heavy armour. Two engines. Longer range. A bit less fast, and we had to carry this chap in the back to work the radio and the machine-gun. We had a name for that feeble gun. It translates as a marmalade thrower. But in front we had two cannon and four machine-guns, all controlled by a switch on the stick. Lovely! You could break up a bomber with one squirt, clear a road, scatter a regiment. After escorting bombers to hit Warsaw or some-where we would break up into a four-plane *Schwarm* to go 'free hunting'. These were lovely days. But you know the real excitement? It was the travel: seeing these Poles; so rural, so backward.

Early in 1940 Hans Kettling took part in the invasion of Norway, with almost fatal consequences:

Our *Staffel* was directed to an airfield supposedly captured by German paratroopers. But the transport planes of para-troopers were diverted by poor weather. When I arrived over the field in the Me 110 the field was still being defended by old RAF Gladiators in the air and troops on the ground. This Gladiator got one of us, and fire from the ground got another. We had no more fuel so we had to strafe the troops on the ground and then go down. We landed, got that marmalade thrower out of the back and started fighting like infantry. A couple of Junkers troop carriers came in and saved us.[2]

Hans Kettling and his fellow pilots were often thinking about the heavy fighting in the south of England:

We were doing our own duty: patrols; chasing a few Blenheims; nothing dramatic. It was fun, deadly fun. But we were content to be out of that other battle. We knew the losses. We knew we had more aircraft. But we also knew that many of your pilots walked home after they were hit. Ours were dead, drowned or, at the very best, prisoners of war. And you could take three damaged Spitfires and make another one. What we lost we lost!

Talking about shooting, Hans said:

I would have shot Ted Shipman without a thought. But I am not a murderer. I was shooting at material. That machinery happened to be operated by a man. But that is only a second thought – a rationalisation. War for us was a sport. It even had rules of a sort. You didn't shoot once the enemy was clearly going down. If he was finished you let him try to land. You didn't shoot at parachutes. Yes, there were a few exceptions. But for most of us this was the way the game was played. If that seems a thoughtless attitude, maybe that was because no one wanted very much to think.

Were we heroes?

Hans answered his own question:

Off duty the job had glamour. It would be a lie to say I did not enjoy to walk the streets in my uniform. But a hero is someone who maybe risks his life to rescue others, not this – a dangerous duty when we had no choice. Some airmen were more special; like my own leader, Helmut Link, who became a great ace. When we would be talking and laughing he would lie on his bed staring. He told me he was thinking about his next attack, going over all alternatives, thinking how things might go wrong, then how he might get away. That is why he was an ace. Not from bravery.

What did we, the British, do? Ted Shipman recalls:

We spent most of time in tents, playing cards, talking. There was no real emotion or apprehension for most of us. A war was on, so what? That's what we trained for. What's to worry about? It showed how little we knew. This attitude did not change until you saw your first German. My first reaction on my first interception was, 'Oh God, it is one of them!' The last thing I wanted to see was those black crosses.

Our training was based on the previous war. The worst memory of that first tangle with the Me 110 was when it came head-on. It was not supposed to do that. Our training had been based on formation flying, and we had assumed that our fleet would sail in and attack their fleet. The chap at the back would do all the fighting. In the event instinct takes over. You try to get behind your man, just like they did in World War I. But at least we had an aircraft capable of the task.

Our Spitfires, given to us in January 1939, were nowhere near as good as those that came later. We had single wooden propellers and you had to pump the wheels up by hand. But it was marvellous. The Spitfire gave you everything you loved about flying – and ten times more. As a fighting machine? We never thought, at the beginning, we would use it for that. It was just a superb aeroplane to fly.

Ted Shipman has no memories of triumphant feeling at success of the first shooting down of an enemy aircraft.

I don't think I have forgotten how I felt. I don't think I felt very much. We had probably killed one or two Germans. It was a big shock. I did not want to talk about it much. We were refused the chance to give the German pilots cigarettes in hospital. I could not understand why. I did not think of them as enemies, Huns, Nazis and all that. They were pilots doing their job, as I was doing mine. That was not a popular view in wartime. But I don't know how many airmen believed all that other Hun stuff anyway.

Our squadron, 41, was moved to Hornchurch for the May 1940 battle of Dunkirk. Untypically in our squadron we had more pilots than Spitfires, so we took it in turns to fly. I flew seven sorties in May over the beaches and I never fired a shot. Another man took my Spitfire in three sorties, and each time the entire squadron got badly beaten up, losing planes and pilots. In June 1940 over the beaches I did see some action. After Dunkirk we positioned in North Yorkshire and were watching the ordeal in the south unfolding. We knew this was the big one. We were feeling a bit edgy. We were expecting to be called down south every day. I suppose most of us were pretty grateful every day that they did not pull us in. I don't think there was too much of the 'if only we could be down there in the thick of it' talk. We had one chap who couldn't sit still, marching up and down outside the tent. Keen to get stuck in or scared? Don't know. No one asked him. Heroes were the odd men out. Blokes like Bader. I knew him – saying they were always dying to get stuck in. They were always on their own. We thought they would call us. We knew we would go. And then we would do all we could. But jumping up and down for a chance? No.

My job was to get in close behind and give the Heinkel or whatever a real good dose. People write about the rattle of the guns. With eight Browning machine-guns firing together it's never a rattle – more like a sustained roar. I was never elated at a success. Some in my squadron took extraordinary pleasure from a kill. Never me. I did not feel guilt because I knew it was them or us.

I was not a hero. We had some successes in our gentle battle. I survived. I can remember the feeling of desperation, not panic, but an acute awareness of the seriousness of the situation. I never was part of the 'tally-ho' or the 'wild-blue-yonder spirit' that some people talk about. There were a lot of carefree individuals in the RAF, yet is carefree the right word? Perhaps they carried too much care, perhaps they felt they had no future beyond the next day or so, and perhaps their attitude was catching, and it came out as this sort of casual heroism. But that was never how it felt ... not when you sat in the cockpit, and got that feeling. Not nerves, not doubts ... but an awareness of the challenge. We weren't totally prepared. Our technical officers had to run around motor factories buying all the rear-view mirrors they could find because our Spits had no way of seeing who was coming up behind.

The battle was not the highlight of my RAF career – my later flying as a staff instructor when I flew over thirty-eight different types of aircraft stays with me as a better memory.

In summary, my part was rather gentle.

How gentle or how ordinary was it possible to be at 15,000 feet with a few seconds in which to kill or die? Hans and Ted were not aces, but not quite like the lives of average men either.[3]

Durham Police were able to turn up a copy of their occurrence book for 15 August 1940, and a transcript of this document is given in Appendix 7.

NOTES

1. The following text was added later by John Shipman, using information given during the interviews for the *Times Saturday Review*, 14 July 1990.
2. Hans Kettling received the Iron Cross in this operation.
3. July edition of *The Times Saturday Review*.

CHAPTER 11

A Perfect Interception

Two patrols and six days later after the big raid on the north, on 21 August 1940 I was standing by at the Greatham forward base as usual with my Green Section of Langley and Usmar. The weather was good, with broken cloud at 9,000 feet, a typical August day.

At 16.08 hours we were ordered to patrol Scarborough at 20,000 feet. Arriving over Scarborough we were sent out to sea on a heading of 110 degrees and were told to reduce to 9,000 feet. This brought us into the layer of broken cumulus cloud. When about fifteen miles out to sea I was told that there was a target two miles ahead flying on the same course. Almost immediately I saw it – a Heinkel 111 dead ahead in a clearing between the heaped clouds – and obviously going home!

I ordered 'line astern', closed to between 200 and 300 yards range, and opened fire. Immediately the mid-upper gunner of the Heinkel opened up on me and I could see the tracer bullets streaking towards me, fortunately passing safely by. I used up 1,444 rounds of ammunition in one long burst. The Heinkel then began to dive, and this enabled the mid-lower gunner to open up, again harmless to me. The effect of my long burst was that the starboard fuel tank between the engine and the fuselage caught fire and the starboard engine poured out white smoke. The aircraft then began a gentle turn to starboard as if to turn back towards land, but this developed into a steep spiral dive down into the sea, the starboard wing breaking off just before impact. I

107

give all credit to the two German gunners, for they continued shooting even in the steep diving spiral. On hitting the sea the Heinkel disappeared in a boiling patch of water, in the centre of which was a patch of blazing fuel. There was no sign of survivors among the few pieces of floating wreckage that were left.

After I had re-formed my section we resumed patrol and were ordered to land at Catterick, which we did at 17.02 hours – just fifty-five minutes after being ordered off.

My log-book entry reads very factually, as follows:

Date and hour	Aeroplane type and No.	Pilot	Time	Duty
Aug 21 12:38	Spitfire I EB L	Self	1:05	Patrol Scarboro' 1 He 111K Shot down.

Much later[1] I discovered the details of the crew[2] of the He 111. They were *Feldwebel* Otto Henkel, aged 25, piloting the He 111, H2 A1 + T which formed part of the 9 *Staffel/Kampfgeschwader* 53 (Condor Legion) *Flieger Korps* II, *Luftflotte* 2, which was based at Lille, north Belgium; *Hauptmann* Georg Ppeiffer, aged 26, navigator and *Staffel Kapitan*; Fritz Ussbaum, aged 23, bomb aimer; *Unteroffizier* Hans Kiank, aged 23, radio operator; Kurt Christ, aged 22, gunner. *Luftwaffe* records show that they were reported missing in Area 2432. This Heinkel came from a unit trained to attack coastal targets and as such normally carried *Kriegsmarine* observers.

de Wilde Ammunition

The introduction of de Wilde ammunition, an incendiary bullet, may well have had the effect of our fighters having a higher rate of more positive 'kills' from the summer of 1940 onwards. But it had the disadvantage of fouling the guns to such an extent that its use was limited to only one gun per aircraft. On my Spitfire it was loaded into No. 1 port gun, and I imagine it was the cause of the starboard fuel tank catching fire on the Heinkel on 21 August.

Transcript of Combat Report Date: 21/8/40

Squadron: 41 (Spitfire) K9805 EB L
Section: Green
Tine: 16.24 hrs
Place: 15 miles east of Scarborough
Aircraft: One Heinkel 111K

Leading Green Section, P/O G.A. Langley and Srgt F. Usmar, I was ordered to patrol Scarborough at 20,000 ft at 16.08 hrs. Taking off from forward base and arriving on patrol, I was ordered to Vector 110 deg. At 9,000 ft. When about 15 miles out to sea, and flying through broken cloud, I was informed that one enemy aircraft was 2 miles ahead of me on the same course. Almost immediately I saw the aircraft, and ordered 'line astern' for an attack.

I opened fire from dead astern at a range of 350 yrds, closing to 200 yrds, and firing 1,444 rounds in one burst. Return fire from the E.A.'s[3] upper fuselage gun was experienced, but without effect. The E.A. did not evade during the attack, but immediately after began to dive and use the bottom fuselage gun, again without effect.

The starboard fuel tank caught fire, the starboard engine emitted white smoke, and the E.A. commenced a turn to starboard as if to return to land. However, the turn developed into a steep spiral dive to starboard, and the aircraft fell vertically into the sea. The starboard wing broke off just before the machine hit the water. The E.A. disappeared completely leaving a patch of blazing fuel on the water, with no trace of survivors.

I reformed my section and continued to patrol until ordered to land. Landed at base at 17.02 hrs.

(Confirmed) Signed: P/O E.A. Shipman.

Heavy Casualties from Squadrons moved from the North to the South[4]

Squadron and Group	Claims	Casualties
41 Squadron, 13 Group	13	1
152 Squadron, 13 Group	4	1
602 Squadron, 13 Group	26	2
266 Squadron, 12 Group	9	6
616 Squadron, 12 Group	8	7

NOTES

1. From Chris Goss, an RAF Cranwell student, who researched some events in the Battle of Britain.
2. *Battle over Britain.*
3. E.A. = Enemy Aircraft.
4. Memorandum from Air Vice-Marshal Keith Park, 26 August 1940. Information provided by Stephen Bungay.

CHAPTER 12

Goodbye Forty-One

On 1 September 1940, while driving back to Catterick after spending the evening with Elsie in Darlington, I was badly shaken in a road accident. It was dark and an air raid warning had sounded. I was driving my Morris Eight quite slowly through Barton village with one passenger, an airman from Dishforth. Having just rounded a sharp bend I saw the dim lights of a vehicle coming towards me from the Catterick direction. As it got near, what appeared to be an army lorry overtook me at high speed, having followed me round the bend. It couldn't get between me and the oncoming car without hitting one of us, and the driver chose me – quite sensibly, I suppose, under the circumstances. The lorry hit my offside front wheel and threw the car onto the nearside kerb, and as luck would have it head-on into a tree which was about a foot behind the kerb. The nearside dumb-iron[1] struck the tree fair and square and deposited me against the steering wheel and the top frame of the windscreen. My passenger was thrown against the top of the windscreen too. We were both slightly dazed, the airman more so as he did not have the benefit of the steering wheel against his stomach. Collecting my wits, I found that the driver of the oncoming car had turned round and was trying to catch the lorry, which didn't stop. However, in the blackout conditions he was unable to do so.

My car was pretty badly damaged in spite of my low speed. The chassis was bent, the front axle and steering twisted, and in addition to the various damage to wings and headlamps, the radiator was pushed back onto the engine. We managed to move the car down a side road and onto the grass verge, and got a lift back to camp. I did not get the car back on the road until the end of November.

The accident left me with a bruised and painful stomach, which kept me off flying for a time, and during this period of non-flying duty the squadron was again sent to Hornchurch. While at Hornchurch the squadron did very well, as on 3 September it claimed seven enemy aircraft for no loss. On 15 September, later known as 'Battle of Britain Day',[2] 41 Squadron worked well with 92 and 222 Squadrons and against high odds (twenty-seven fighters against a formation of 474 enemy aircraft). I felt pretty upset at this, and was even more upset when about a week later I was posted to flying instructor duties and went to Montrose. So on 25 September I was flown to No. 8 SFTS[3] in a Blenheim of 219 Squadron.

Although Fighter Command never had enough aircraft or pilots for the tasks they were given, in number there were usually more pilots available than aircraft. In 41 Squadron, for instance, our strengths were as follows:

	Aircraft Serviceable	Aircraft Unserviceable	Pilots
1/7/40	11	6	21
1/8/40	10	6	19
1/9/40	14	3	20

The overall position for Fighter Command on the evening of 6 September 1940 was 750 serviceable aircraft and 1,381 pilots, of whom about 950 were either Spitfire or Hurricane pilots. Despite casualties Fighter Command was growing in strength, with about 200 more pilots and about 150 more aircraft than were available at the beginning of July 1940.[4]

Being based at Catterick, we were less actively engaged than were those squadrons further south, and our trips to Hornchurch were to relieve them. Their casualty rates were much higher.

Between the beginning of Dunkirk and 1 September, 41 Squadron lost only one pilot and seven aircraft, mainly at Hornchurch during the first two detachments there. However, between 1 September and 30 October the squadron lost nine pilots killed and nine wounded, and thirty-six aircraft – mainly in September.

Against the squadron's total losses of thirty-seven aircraft and ten pilots killed, the enemy lost thirty-nine aircraft. Of course, their crews would all be lost, too, either killed or taken prisoner.

A lot of the fighting was at high altitude, and the Spitfires were hard pushed to reach the incoming enemy aircraft. To reach altitudes of 37,500 feet took too long, and once there the Spitfire was at its maximum ceiling, with poor stability and control. The enemy aircraft had superior two-stage supercharged engines which compressed more oxygen into the cylinders. Icing of the canopy and the pilot's oxygen supply at this altitude was also a problem. Opening the hood to see at these altitudes brought additional problems of extreme cold.

I missed out on further front-line action, including some battles in which colleagues lost their lives or were injured. Three such encounters that I missed are described below.

G.H. 'BEN' BENNIONS

One of our pilots who was badly injured was Plt Off G.H. Bennions,[5] who lost an eye with a canon shell exploding in his cockpit. He baled out and became one of Archibald MacIndoe's guinea pigs in plastic surgery. I later met him at Catterick in 1942, when he was Operations Officer.

Bennions was preparing to go on leave and he was wearing his best uniform, ready to depart, when he was scrambled to intercept a force of Messerschmitt fighters at 20,000 feet just north of Brighton. He shot down one before a cannon shell exploded in the cockpit of his Spitfire, blinding him in the left eye and severely damaging his right arm and leg.

Bleeding profusely, badly burned and with the median nerve to his right hand severed, he struggled to get out of his Spitfire, and eventually succeeded in opening his parachute before losing consciousness. He was found in a field, and quickly taken to Horsham hospital for emergency treatment. The rapid intervention of an eye surgeon saved his right eye, but it was too late to save the left. A few days later Bennions was transferred to Queen Victoria Hospital, East Grinstead, where he became one of the first pilots to come under the care of Sir Archibald McIndoe, the plastic surgeon who pioneered the treatment for severe burns. Bennions became one of 'Archie's Guinea Pigs', the name which the severely burned or otherwise disfigured casualties gave themselves. Later, McIndoe's patients formed the Guinea Pig Club; Bennions was a founder member. By using a parachute to save his life, he had also become eligible for membership of the Caterpillar Club.

Bennions's time as a patient at East Grinstead had a profound effect on him. Years later, he wrote of his feelings at the time: 'Flying had meant everything to me. I had lost an eye, couldn't even write or walk, and felt that my whole life was finished. But Archie was such a marvellous man, and seeing people around me who were much worse off than I was gave me a sense of proportion.' Once he had recovered from his serious injuries, Bennions regained a limited flying category, but was unable to fly in combat. He became a fighter controller in the north of England, and was promoted to squadron leader.

'Robin' Hood

On 5 September 1940 Squadron Leader 'Robin' Hood led twelve Spitfires of 41 Squadron from Hornchurch with orders to patrol Maidstone at 15,000 feet. 'Robin' flew as Blue 1 of 'B' Flight, and rearguard cover was provided by 'A' Flight, led by Flt Lt Norman Ryder. The scramble was a hurried event, and as the squadron was still climbing away from Hornchurch a large enemy formation was encountered flying up the Thames estuary towards London. This formation consisted of Heinkel 111s, Dornier 17s and Junkers 88s, all escorted by Me 109s. Other Fighter Command squadrons had been vectored to intercept this raid, including Hurricanes of North Weald's 249 Squadron, Debden's 17 and 73 Squadrons, Northolt's 303 Squadron and Stapleford's 46 Squadron.

'Wally' Wallens

Pilot Officer 'Wally' Wallens was flying as Number 2 to 'Robin' Hood, and being unable to gain sufficient height advantage and position, 'Robin' put 'B' Flight into line astern and open-echelon port and ordered a head-on attack: a desperate and scary manoeuvre, but the only possible one under the circumstances. 'B' Flight was overwhelmed by the Me 109s as all hell broke loose.

'Wally' Wallens broke away after firing at the bombers on a collision course, and escaped the Me 109s by diving to 10,000 feet and then climbing nearly as steeply again to gain the advantage of height. 'Wally' caught up with two Me 109s which were returning home in open formation. He attacked one with a long burst which destroyed it, and then slid in behind the second Me 109. As soon as this manoeuvre was complete 'Wally' realised his mistake – he should have broken away. A third Me 109 was covering the first two, and this one screamed in on the Spitfire and fired at long range. The Me 109 cannon shells ripped into the Spitfire and took great chunks out of the wings, the instrument panel disintegrated with the radio, the armoured-glass windscreen was scored on the inside and 'Wally's' leg went numb as a shell tore into it. The hood was jammed, so a bale-out was not possible. With a faltering engine 'Wally' limped to within four miles of Hornchurch before the engine ceased and a forced landing was made. Farm workers on the ground helped to release the hood and lift 'Wally' clear. On further inspection 'Wally' noticed that a radio earpiece and his wristwatch had been shot to pieces. The thick armour behind the seat in the Spitfire had almost been penetrated by cannon shells, and they were still embedded there. Hospitalisation took 'Wally' out of the front line.[6]

Four of the twelve Spitfires from 41 Squadron failed to return. Plt Off Tony 'Lulu' Lovell had parachuted out of his burning aircraft over South Benfleet and returned to Hornchurch. Flt Lt Webster was killed and 'Robin' Hood was posted as missing. Eyewitnesses reported a collision between a Spitfire and another British aircraft. Although it was thought that two Spitfires from 41 had collided (Webster and Hood), it now seems more likely that Webster collided with Flt Lt Lovell's Hurricane. Webster's seat was found by one farmer (Walter Smith), while another (Roland Wilson) found the tail section, and then some weeks later he found an unopened parachute marked 'WEBSTER'.

Two young children (Sam and Brenda Armfield) found a Spitfire fuselage which lacked the engine and a portion of the port wing nearby. There were no bullet holes in it and no blood in the cockpit. This may have been 'Robin' Hood's Spitfire 'EB-R'. It is thought that 'Robin' Hood baled out, but his parachute became entangled with his aircraft as his Spitfire (P9428) tumbled down, engineless and minus its port wing.[7]

It is thought that 'Robin' Hood's body was unrecognisable and that he was buried by mistake in a German pilot's grave within Becontree Cemetery (B1: 684 12 September 1940).[8]

There were many casualties, and the collection of bodies were transferred to Hornchurch by the local undertaker (Mr Green of Frank Rivett and Sons) for distribution and burial.

NOTES

1. Dumb-iron is part of the chassis just above the spring hanger behind the bumper.
2. This was the day when all available fighting resources were pressed into action and Churchill, observing the action from Uxbridge Operations Room, learnt that there were no reserves.
3. Service Flying Training School.
4. Information provided by Stephen Bungay.
5. Bennions was shot down on 17 September 1940 while attacking forty Me 109s on his own at 30,000 feet. He claimed one aircraft, taking his total of confirmed victories to twelve, with five additional probables. Hit in the arm, leg and head, Bennions parachuted to safety and spent five weeks undergoing surgery.
6. Information supplied by 'Wally' Wallens from his book, *Flying Made My Arms Ache*.
7. Description from a *Luftwaffe* combat report and claim 1/JG54.
8. Some information from the book, *Missing In Action – Resting in Peace?*, By Dilip Sarkar.

CHAPTER 13

Moving On

The pilot and aircrew training scheme was getting well under way by late 1940, and there was a great need for operationally trained and experienced pilots to become instructors. Although the squadrons were naturally loath to part with their trained pilots, it was realised that they must let a 'trickle' go to Training Command in order to get the adequately trained new pilots and aircrew into the squadrons from the schools.

I had left an active 41 Squadron at RAF Catterick in September 1940 to join other pilots who were deemed to be essential to provide pilot training for the coming months and possibly years of the war. No. 41 Squadron was still in the thick of the Battle of Britain when I left, and I often wonder what my fate might have been had I not been posted to other duties. There was a degree of sadness when one had to leave the excitement of squadron life and the interceptions in Spitfires, but to balance this there was the realisation that the chances of survival were obviously greater when away from the front line and the dangerous dog-fights of the skies. I was never one to shirk my duty at the sharp end of the war.

Historians[1] have examined the Battle of Britain period and have produced some interesting, revealing and frightening statistics (see Table below). The average RAF pilot rarely got more than twenty-four hours off in seven days, or seven days off in three months. In terms of flying hours, an RAF fighter pilot's life could be calculated as eighty-seven hours. The Air Ministry estimated that every fighter pilot kept in action for more than six months would be shot down due to exhaustion, or staleness, or because he had lost the will to fight.

117

The new challenges of pilot training chosen for me by the Air Ministry were to eventually turn out as being more rewarding and just as important as chasing enemy aircraft up and down the coast of Yorkshire or Kent.

Battle of Britain: July–October period

Average RAF Pilot Strength 1,484	RAF aircraft serviceability 608

Losses 10 July to 31 October

	RAF	*Luftwaffe*
Aircraft	1,449	1,733
Pilots	903	2,698
	(415 killed, 66 missing or POW, 422 wounded)	
Number of sorties	42,895 (8 days in September unrecorded)	?

2,917 RAF pilots had flown one or more sorties
452 RAF pilots went through the whole Battle
217 RAF pilots were operational at outbreak of war

25 SEPTEMBER 1940, No. 8 SERVICE FLYING TRAINING SCHOOL – MONTROSE, SCOTLAND

The new RAF pilot and aircrew training scheme was getting well under way by late 1940. The formal training of instructors was to form the basis of instruction the world over in a few years, right throughout the military and the civilian sectors. Some pilots were specially selected to train pilots who would themselves become instructors – thereby accelerating the numbers of qualified pilots who would then be available for combat and other duties.

Although we had many interruptions during night-flying due to air raid warnings, the only real enemy activity we experienced was one Saturday afternoon when shopping in Montrose: a hit-and-run raider machine-gunned the streets, but fortunately there were no casualties. Elsie and I took cover in a doorway during this attack. After this a section of fighters was put on standby on the airfield.

We lost two pupils during solo night-flying. One flew into the sea while overshooting from a bad approach and landing. The other appeared to lose sight of the aerodrome lights and got lost. In spite of an extensive search we never found him, and we imagine he ended up in the sea, too. What was found during this search on the top of the Grampians was a wrecked WWI plane with the remains of the pilot in the cockpit!

So after less than four months at Montrose I was back at CFS at Upavon, this time to train flying instructors. These pilots would then, hopefully, train other pilots.

Avro Tutors, Harvards, Miles Masters with Rolls Kestrel engines and later Master IIIs with American Wasp engines were our aircraft. Soon after my arrival I managed to get a trip in the one and only Spitfire we had at CFS. Then on 1 April 1941, just a year after being commissioned, I was made a substantive flying officer.

Now began my experience with many foreign air force pilots, and the difficulties of understanding and making myself understood, although on the whole the majority of these chaps could speak English fairly well, and some, of course, very well. There were French, Dutch, Poles, Czechs and Greeks, and the work was, to say the least, most interesting, if somewhat exasperating at times.

EMPIRE CENTRAL FLYING SCHOOL (ECFS)

On 24 February 1943 I was posted to the Empire Central Flying School for No. 4 Course, and was rated as 'exceptional' both as a pilot and as an instructor. The objects of the ECFS course, which lasted three months, were to get together experienced officers from all the allied air forces and the various branches of the RAF, to pool and exchange their knowledge and broaden their outlook, especially in up-to-date operational requirements. All students had to have done at least one tour of operations or more than 1,000 hours as a flying instructor, and had to be suitable for executive posts.

My first task on the course was to get the other members of my group off in all the aircraft we were to fly, to which they were strangers. In the three months of the course, flying was done in twelve different aircraft. Much of the flying was designed to make the student more critical and analytical of instructional methods and of aircraft performance. Many specialist lectures were given, and regular visits were made to operational units in the field and to aircraft factories. Regular debates were held, and by the end of the course recommendations for the improvement of the many aspects of instructional and operational flying were produced for direct submission to the Air Ministry. When it was all over I was relieved to hear that I had been awarded the highest assessment – a Special Distinction, and then followed the news that I was to go to Southern Rhodesia as a squadron leader chief flying instructor at the Rhodesian CFS.

NOTE

1. Derek Woods and Derek Dempster, *The Narrow Margin*.

CHAPTER 14

Journey to Southern Rhodesia

The last few days of my leave were spent at my father's farm, Eaton Lodge. Completing my goodbyes, I returned to Hullavington on Thursday 10 June 1943. The next evening I was on the train for West Kirby in the Wirral. We arrived at 17.45 hours, where, with many others, I drew the essential tropical kit (standard issue), in which I felt and looked terrible. Luggage was repacked and marked in accordance with embarkation instructions showing destination, route and ship, in code, of course – LJLJ C3/M in my case. All officers were issued with .38 revolvers and twelve rounds of ammunition. We left by train for Gourock early on 17 June 1943. There were about 400 airmen on my draft, with two other officers. We arrived at Gourock at 11.15 hours. After some delay because of congestion of tenders embarking other troops, we eventually pulled alongside a large grey ship[1] and went aboard at 13.45 hours. I found myself berthed in a two-berth cabin with seven other RAF officers.

My particular responsibility was C2 Aft Deck, which housed one flight sergeant, four sergeants. and 171 airmen. Our ship was American and civilian owned and operated. It was built at Hamburg for the north Atlantic run, and of course as such was quite unsuitable for tropical conditions. After two boat drills we moved off at 21.30 hours in a convoy of seven ships. That first night I did duty watch below on the airmen's deck. The next morning, Sunday 20 June, at 09.00 hours, we were leaving the coast behind. The convoy[2] was now twelve ships plus a cruiser and several destroyers. Other ships in the convoy were the *Clan Macarthur*, *John Ericsson* (US), and the *Stratheden*. The ships continually zigzagged to combat the U-boat threat.

During the first two days we steamed north, then north-west, and following this, westerly, then south-westerly and finally southerly. We knew we must be well out into the Atlantic, for we had to put our clocks and watches back one hour. The poor food and water supplies on the overcrowded ship resulted in many sick people. On 1 July we steamed into Freetown, on the coast of Sierra Leone. Being only about nine degrees north of the equator, Freetown was very hot and humid, and we were glad to be able to spend more time on the open decks and not blacked-out for a change. The main attraction was watching natives paddling round the ship in their small boats trying to sell fresh fruit and diving for 'Glasgow Tanners' (pennies – sometimes wrapped in tin foil from cigarette packets – or silver threepenny pieces) thrown into the water from the white-faced watchers above. In this latter pursuit they were very successful, which indicated much practice and no doubt profit from many previous ships. Finally, on Tuesday 6 July, after five days' delay, we were away and going south again.

SURVIVORS AND BOAT DRILL

When about seventy miles out, our attention was drawn to one of the escorting destroyers[3] turning and stopping to pick up nearly thirty survivors from a drifting lifeboat. Their ship had been torpedoed four days earlier.[4]

CAPE TOWN

On Wednesday 21 July at 15.20 hours we arrived at Cape Town after the usual degaussing operation in the open waters of the harbour. This was a procedure which all shipping had to do as a protection against magnetic mines. We disembarked and were taken to the transit camp, named the 'Retreat', where we spent two days sorting out baggage once again and organising the troops for their dispersal to their various destinations. The rail trip to Salisbury took almost four days, with three nights spent on the train. The distance being some 1,600 miles, we managed an average speed of about fifteen miles per hour, excluding stops, of which there were many, to drop off and pick up native passengers.

My arrival in Salisbury on 1 August was followed by an interview the next day at the Rhodesian Air Training Group HQ (RAT Group) regarding my posting. Although I had been posted for duty as a squadron leader at the CFS at Norton, and indeed had a copy of the authority in my pocket, I was astonished and most disappointed to be told that a Rhodesian officer had been promoted to the post. Naturally I protested and suggested that I should be sent back home. My case was referred back to the Air Ministry, which instructed that I was to be employed as a flight lieutenant, but only at CFS.

NORTON

Arriving at my destination, I found that Norton was No. 33 Flying Instructors' School, and not CFS, but it made no difference for the work was just the same. The August weather, to me at any rate, was hot in spite of the fact that almost the whole of the country was 4,000 feet above sea level. There was none of the English cloud, and the sun beat down relentlessly from morning till night. This cloudless sky extended from about March or the beginning of April to August or September, when small amounts of cloud would form each afternoon, getting more extensive day by day, until by December the atmosphere became very oppressive, with increasingly thundery conditions. Then the rains came in semi-tropical torrents until the end of February. These heavy summer rains were a welcome change to the oppressive spring, and when the weather cleared, the air was wonderfully fresh and sweet – a most exhilarating atmosphere. I was told that Rhodesians considered it essential to have a coastal holiday every year and that Rhodesia had an extremely high suicide rate.

DOWN TO WORK

Within the first few days of arriving at Norton I realised what a different and difficult task it would be to put across to the new instructors we were teaching the new training ideas we had learned and accepted at ECFS and which were based on experience gained in the operational squadrons which were fighting the war. I found that the majority of the staff, from the CO downwards, had no current operations experience in the European theatre. My difficulties were made worse by not having the promotion and appointment for which I was posted. However, I was determined to 'press on' with the job, and over the months that followed I managed to gradually convert, to some degree, quite a few of my fellow instructors. Engine handling for efficiency, simple experimental flying to know the aeroplane better, and experience in flying it to its limit with safety were all part of the new doctrine I was introducing.

Our aircraft at that time were Tiger Moths for elementary instructors, and Harvards and Oxfords for the service instructors. This new flight became known as the CFS Flight, and the station's name was changed to CFS (Southern Rhodesia).

Very soon after forming the CFS Flight, and just about one year after arriving at Norton, I was promoted to squadron leader and took over as Assistant Chief Flying Instructor. In no time at all we were using new training techniques, including 'two-stage blue' to turn those bright cloudless skies into dark night conditions, which really made the chaps sweat and work really hard to fly 'through the overcast' on instruments alone.

TWO-STAGE BLUE – AN EXPLANATION

During the war, in England, air raids and weather interfered considerably with the training of pilots in flying at night. Flare-paths and training aircraft flying round airfields were vulnerable to enemy bombers and intruding long-range fighters, and bad weather added to the frustration of achieving adequate night-flying for training purposes. This problem was fully appreciated in the early days of the war, and in 1942, at the Empire Central Flying School at Hullavington, research was started into achieving night conditions during daylight, which was a little safer.

In the first scheme a flare-path of sodium light was put out on the airfield, and the pilot wore a pair of goggles with a light filter which would admit only sodium light. This meant that he could see only the sodium lights of the flare path, so the cockpit instruments had to be illuminated by sodium light. As this method was quite successful, it was put into general use and allowed valuable 'night-flying' training to be done in broad daylight. To the pilot the main problem was the cumbersome and heavy goggles he had to wear.

The second scheme got rid of the flare-path by fitting amber screens to the inside of the cockpit windscreens and windows and giving the pilot goggles with amber lenses complementary to the amber screens. The combination of the screens and goggle lenses reduced the amount of light reaching the pilot's eyes but still allowed him to see his instruments. Varying the density of the goggle lenses varied the degree of 'night' effect. Again this scheme was a success, although there was some criticism of the amber hue which surrounded the pilot. Both these two-stage schemes allowed quite realistic conditions of vision at night to be experienced – full-moon light with light lenses, through increasing darkness, to almost a totally black night with the darkest lenses. Ordinary installed runway lighting could be seen adequately, so a special flare-path like the sodium one was not necessary.

OUR TIRED OLD AIRCRAFT

In Rhodesia, flying from ground level, which was between 4,000 and 4,500 feet above sea level, our training was getting tedious and wasteful. The Tiger Moths were getting old and took a long time to climb to a safe aerobatic height, which in effect was about 7,000 feet above sea level. The Oxfords, on the other hand, had worn-out Cheetah engines. The Cheetahs had poor cylinder compression due to badly worn piston rings. Only the Harvards were keeping pace with the calendar.

The solution to our problems came in two ways – American Ryan Cornells to replace the Tigers, and new engines, Pratt and Whitney Twin Wasp Juniors with variable-pitch propellers, for the Oxfords. These gave us a much better performance with the Oxford, with the facility to teach more advanced engine handling. However, the increased power of the Wasp engines and the higher airspeeds exposed and brought about other trouble. The Oxford's all-wood construction began to suffer from glue failure. Many months of exposure to extreme changes of temperature by day and night caused a serious reduction in the strength of the glued joints. It was unfortunate that this defect was not discovered until one of the Oxfords from nearby Heany broke up in the air, killing the occupants. An immediate inspection of all Oxfords revealed several other cases of approaching failure.

COURTS OF INQUIRY

Crashes occur and they have to be investigated. In Rhodesia it was customary for the CFI at CFS to head the courts of inquiry into fatal crashes at other training schools, and it became my lot to be given this job on several occasions.

The first one was when a Harvard from Cranborne crashed near a farm during a solo flight, killing the pupil. Taking evidence from natives was usually an exasperating and difficult business, and we had to be careful to assess how much was truth, how much exaggeration or pure romance, or even fright! Of course the real object of the inquiry was to find the cause of the accident, whether technical, pilot error or perhaps a fault or an omission in training methods.

In this particular case the cause of the Harvard crash did not become clear until we managed to find several natives who were sure the aeroplane (the 'big bird' as they called it) was attacking the farm. It transpired that the pupil concerned had spent the last weekend as a guest at that same farm, and no doubt was 'showing off' to his hosts.

Another crash worth recounting concerned an Oxford from the SFTS at Kumalo, near Bulawayo. This aircraft broke up in the air while doing instrument flying some distance from the aerodrome. Both the instructor and pupil were killed, and the bits of the aircraft were scattered over several square miles of the bush (or 'bundu', as the natives called it).

Four of us spent some two days searching the bush to find important bits of the Oxford. The bush was so dense in parts that we had to use compasses to avoid getting lost ourselves. Having got all the pieces we could find, we laid them out on a hangar floor and tried to put them together – an almost impossible task because so many small bits were missing.

One of our instructors was Peter Chiswell, an arty sort of chap and an accomplished cartoonist, who from time to time drew for *Punch* under the name of 'Dit', and frequently kept us amused with his drawings. He saw the funny side of the most ordinary everyday event, and would produce a quick cartoon, while drinking his morning cup of coffee, of some incident that had happened in the air with his pupil. Scarcely a day passed without a quick sketch being done.[5]

He produced Christmas cards for us and graphic aids to instruction, and on the occasions of staff meetings, which were usually held in the education section, the blackboard would be the means of depicting the typical 'goon' pupil, who might be captioned facetiously as 'a keen smiling type who should do well'. Peter, while being a capable instructor, was quite absent minded, and this was his downfall at Norton. Soon after we had the Oxfords fitted with the Wasp engines, he took one to Bulawayo, intending to get back just before dusk. He became overdue on his return flight, and although we called him continuously on the very limited radio equipment we had, there was no reply. It was getting dark, so we put out the flare-path and we checked with Kumalo to verify that he had left on time – and waited. Eventually, after a period of tense listening and looking, when it was evident that he could no longer be in the air, we notified Group that he was missing and packed up for the night – an uneasy night, to say the least. There was nothing we could do until daybreak.

The next day a general air search was organised to cover his route, but without result. All enquiries were negative, too. It was a day or so later that news came in of his safety – he had overshot Norton through not realising the higher airspeed of the Wasp-powered Oxford, and computing the Cheetah-powered Oxford speed for the flight time. Not finding Norton when his planned flight time had elapsed, he searched until running out of fuel, then he baled-out in the near darkness. After landing he became scared stiff by hearing growling animal noises coming out of the surrounding bush, and he lost no time in climbing the nearest tree, where he spent the night.

In the morning Peter decided to walk in a direction which he thought might lead him to some habitation. Little did he know that he was in fact miles from any farmstead or native village, but he was amazingly lucky, for after walking only a short distance he came across some recently made vehicle tracks in the long grass. Turning along the track in the direction he though the vehicle had gone, luck was with him again, for he walked into a government surveyor's camp and discovered that the man was only in this particular area once a year for one day too! Having been given the area of the crash, we never found the Oxford from the air, in spite of its bright yellow colour, and it took a troop of askaris nearly a week to locate it. This difficulty in finding a brightly coloured, crashed aircraft in bush country is quite common; on another occasion a Tiger Moth which crashed within close sight of its aerodrome at Mount Hampden was not found for over a week.

CANNIBALS

A much less fortunate end befell the crew of another Oxford from one of the twin-engined FTSs near Bulawayo. Two pupils were doing a solo triangular cross-country flight and failed to return. Some days later it was found that their aircraft had landed relatively safely well to the west in the uninhabited Kalahari Desert, but there were no signs of the two cadets. A closer examination of the Oxford showed that the magnetic compass had been removed and the first-aid kit was missing. Hopes for the safety of the cadets rose as the discovery indicated that they had used their initiative and were trying to reach help.

Nothing was heard of the two cadets for a very long time until a report was received from the South African Police that traces of service clothing and equipment had been found in a bushmen's camp. This tribe of bushmen were known to be cannibals, and it was suspected that the two unfortunate airmen had met their awful fate at the hands of these natives. Later, several of these bushmen were charged with the murder of the airmen.

We presumed the pilots had got lost and had run out of fuel. The presence of mind of the two unfortunates in removing the compass from the aircraft was much to their credit; however, having taken the compass from the aircraft, they forgot to make allowance for the very different reading it would give when not affected by the metal in the aircraft, for which adjustments had been made when it was installed. This error in the compass reading caused them to walk away from civilisation and help rather than towards it.

HURRICANES AT NORTON

In July 1944 we had managed to get several Hurricanes which had been in the Middle East. They were pretty well clapped out, and had to be carefully checked and serviced. We used them for communication and to give the instructors advanced experience. Later in October, Group Headquarters held a flypast of Hurricanes at Cranborne in which I took part.

The following year, when Victory in Europe (VE) Day had come and gone and the end of the war in other parts of the world was in sight, I felt that my instructors particularly, and if possible those pupils who wished to do so, should be allowed to have a trip in the Hurricanes. The majority did, and flew the aircraft very well. There was one unfortunate accident, however, and that was to one of my more experienced instructors, who dived vertically into the ground from a considerable height. Of course, the cause of the crash was never known. It could well have been anoxia if the chap had gone too high without oxygen. The fact that he did not attempt to bale-out or control the dive rather indicates that he was unconscious.

VICTORIA FALLS

In nearly two and a half years in Rhodesia I had one weekend in Bulawayo and eight days' leave which I took at the Victoria Falls.

The visit to the Falls was, of course, a memorable one. Moving into the rain forest a little to the north-east along the edge of the gorge, you need a mackintosh, for the trees are dripping as though it is a pouring-wet day. This is continuous and is due to the condensing of the vapour which rises like steam from the gorge. The vapour has been given the native title 'Mosi-Oa Tunya' (smoke that thunders).

The hotel was plagued by baboons which came onto the large lawn from the surrounding trees to steal sugar, milk and cakes that might be left on the vacant tea tables. They even climbed onto the iron balconies of the bedrooms, and would nip into the hotel rooms to steal if the chance arose.

Just before the annual rains we used to be bothered by 'rain-birds', which are a species of stork, black and white in colour, with a wingspan of six or seven feet. They could be a serious risk to our aircraft as they usually congregated in their scores on the aerodrome. We had one Harvard damaged by a rain-bird when landing; the poor bird was killed.

THE AIR FORCE CROSS

On the morning of 1 January 1945 a personal signal from the SASO, Air Commodore L.H. Cockley, informed me, with his congratulations, that I had been decorated with the Air Force Cross. However, I was not to receive the cross for some three and a half years, and was not to know what the citation said until seven years later. Of course I was allowed and expected to wear the ribbon immediately.

BATTLE OF BRITAIN FLYPAST

Our flying was going to end soon. The Rhodesian Air Training Group decided to mark the cessation of flying training in the Colony with a commemorative flypast of Hurricanes over Salisbury on 15 September, Battle of Britain Day. I was asked to lead Blue Section, and after some minor trouble with aircraft serviceability, we managed to put on quite a good show, with six aircraft in two flights of three, an event which seemed to be much appreciated.

THE END OF CENTRAL FLYING SCHOOL (SR) NORTON

All flying ceased on 7 September 1945. The aircraft had gone to the ARD at Heany, or, in the case of American aircraft, which were 'lend-lease', to the Union of South Africa, and all but a small skeleton staff were posted, mainly to the UK. I was given the task of finally closing the station down and handing it over to the civil authorities for use as a camp for the Italian prisoners of war, who would be deported.

The job completed, we left Norton on 13 October and went to Cranborne. In the meantime I had received my posting signal for my return home – back to ECFS at Hullavington to become a course tutor. I was delighted and could not have wished for a better post, for I was familiar with the work and enjoyed the atmosphere of that unusual and important station.

So it was back on the train for another two days to Durban, which we reached six days after leaving Salisbury. At Durban there was again no opportunity for sightseeing or shopping, for the train drew up on the dockside next to the ship – the *Cape Town Castle*, which was the Union-Castle flagship, and we went straight on board. It was a nice ship but was not in good condition because of trooping and moving a lot of Italian POWs.

We sailed the next morning, 6 November, at 09.30 hours, but not before 'the lady in white' had sung to us in the customary way. I had heard of her from the chaps in Rhodesia, for, unknown by name, she had entertained every ship of troops arriving at or departing from Durban throughout the war. She was elegantly dressed in white from head to foot and sang, unaccompanied, those traditional and patriotic songs commonly heard during the war. She was a typical operatic singer, a great favourite, and she became a legend with the troops.

We headed north leaving the African continent on our left, and headed to the Suez Canal. After picking up more troops and civilians we steamed out of the Suez Canal and into the Mediterranean in the evening of the 20th. By the evening of the 22nd we could see the lights of Malta to the south, and early the next morning we were off Cape Bon. We were now making a good speed and passed our sister ship at 10.30 hours on 23 November, and at this time we were reported to be three hours behind schedule. When we passed Gibraltar early on 24 November we had made up a lot of time. Twenty-four hours later we turned north for the last stretch home and towards a rough English Channel. A gale was blowing when we entered it at 07.00 hours on 27 November, but the bad weather did not seem to matter at this stage, as we were by now quite seasoned sailors and, above all, we were nearly home!

We cleared customs and obtained railway warrants from the movement's office, and so began the last lap by a rather tedious train journey to Darlington.

NOTES

1. Probably the *John Ericsson* (US) in Convoy WS 31. Information from Mike Holdoway. http://www.convoyweb.org.uk
2. Convoy No. KMF 17.

3. HMS *Wolverine*.
4. On 2 July 1943, 150 miles south-west of Monrovia and 250 miles SW of Freetown, the unescorted cargo ship *Empire Kohinoor*, 5,231 tons (Ministry Of War Transport, Anchor Line, managers), on passage from the Table Bay, Middle East, to the UK, was sunk by U-618. Six crew members were lost. The master, seventy-two crew members and eight gunners were rescued. The first boat was rescued by destroyer HMS *Wolverine*, which landed survivors at Takoradi. The second boat was rescued by the British merchantman *Gascony*, and the third lifeboat landed at Lumley Beach, Sierra Leone, on 7 July. Source: Mark Gamble.
5. Peter Chiswell became South Africa's most famous radio personality during the 1950s and 1960s. South Africa did not get television till the mid-70s, so Peter Chiswell was a household name on the radio. He was an incredible man. He wrote, produced, directed, presented and acted in many a radio show, and even composed and played the music for programmes, many of which were enormously popular. It was while on leave in Cape Town that he met his future wife. Her father was a captain in the Navy and was obliged to entertain the visiting RAF pilot. When Peter returned to South Africa, with no formal training save for being a talented musician, well versed in English literature and possessing a sharp wit, on the recommendation of his father-in-law he decided to try his hand in radio. A natural entertainer, he became immensely popular, or, some might say, notorious.

CHAPTER 15

ECFS Again

After the usual twenty-eight days' disembarkation leave spent between Darlington and Eaton Lodge, I left Elsie at Darlington and reported for duty at Hullavington once again. It was about a month later that I managed to get rooms at the sub-post office and village store at Langley Burrell, which was convenient for both Hullavington and Chippenham.

Settling in to the job of tutor at ECFS was easy, as I was familiar with both the work and the ideas of the place. My first students came from the RAF, Canada and South Africa. They were rather fewer than usual, so I had time to fly with other students occasionally and to gain experience and qualification on additional aircraft, such as the Lancaster, Wellington, Mosquito, Mitchell, Stimpson Reliant, Hotspur glider, Bristol Buckmaster, *Rhönbussard* sailplane, Percival Prentice and Gloster Meteor.

One of my RAF students, Flt Lt Ken Tapper, specialised in all-weather flying, with the result that he was taken on the staff, promoted to squadron leader, wrote a pamphlet, 'Flight Through Instruments', and was awarded the MBE. I was pleased to be able to help towards his efforts in small practical ways, especially in producing a flying instrument layout to be photographed for the pamphlet. Ken eventually became the chief instructor at CFS Little Rissington as a wing commander.

THE TUTOR

Life as a tutor at ECFS was demanding but interesting and rewarding. There was little free time, as the tutor was responsible in the widest sense for his student's work, flying of course, but also written work, attendance at lectures and project work in which they were all expected to partake. The tutor was looked upon as a guide, mentor and friend, especially to those students from overseas or from other services. We were expected to attend all main lectures, debates and the daily meteorological briefings (which students had to give in the latter half of their course), and, unless more urgently engaged, to sit in for many of the specialist lectures and demonstrations with our own students – in fact virtually working with them all the time.

Flt Lt Oldmeadow had one leg and refused to wear an artificial one. Flt Lt McKeard used to fly the Lancaster into as many thunderstorms as he could find. Flt Lt Ken Tapper, my star pupil, later became CFI at CFS Little Rissington. Flt Lt Chinnory later became ADC to Prince Philip. Capt 'Birdie' Partridge sank the German cruiser *Königsberg* on 9 April 1940 during a bombing attack involving sixteen Blackburn Skuas of 800 Naval Air Squadron. He also shot down a Heinkel 111 on 27 April 1940, and after crash-landing on a frozen fjord escaped back to his ship. Later he was involved in the attempt to sink the German battle cruisers *Scharnhorst* and *Gneisenau* in Trondheim harbour. His aircraft blew up, and though badly burned he baled-out, was captured and spent five years as a POW.

THE AERONAUTICAL LABORATORY

One of our attractive and useful assets was a well-equipped aeronautical laboratory, which contained a 3 ft diameter wind tunnel and other apparatus for experimenting and teaching in aerodynamics. The laboratory was to provide the students with information concerning the theme of the week: for instance, the first week the subject would be ECFS itself, its work, aims, the different departments and the main personalities; then, during successive weeks, the themes would be the various RAF commands, e.g. Bomber, Fighter, Coastal, etc., then the Army, Navy, each Commonwealth country and finally the various specialist subjects in turn, such as engines, aircraft development, navigation, etc.

END-OF-COURSE RECOMMENDATIONS

Improvements in pilot-training techniques resulted from our research, discussion and recommendations. Towards the end of each course more and more time would be devoted to preparing recommendations for discussion and debate for final accept-ance and passing direct to the Air Ministry for consideration and hopefully adoption. This was a unique opportunity for us, the users in the field, to put our opinions and requirements to the powers at the top without them being vetoed, watered down or altered by the staff officers at the intermediate levels of Group and Command. Every single recommendation was debated and voted on in three separate stages, and an adequate majority had to be obtained at each stage. This ensured that only serious and well-supported ideas ever got a chance of getting through.

THE END-OF-COURSE MAIN LECTURE

The final lecture at the end of each course was an opportunity for either the Assistant Chief of the Air Staff for Training, or some other equally important officer, to come down from the Air Ministry and cast some 'pearls of wisdom', and usually give some thoughts on future official policy. But what was perhaps equally important was that such a visit gave us and our students the chance to put our visitor 'on the spot'. Questions could be asked and views expressed which could never be put on paper. The rules were 'no holds barred', and anyone could say exactly what he liked without fear of getting into trouble for his opinion. Sometimes the views of a most junior student could have great effect, such as on one occasion when the visitor was Air Chief Marshal Sir Basil Embry.

It was at the time when the fighter squadrons were being re-equipped with jet aircraft, and a flight lieutenant expressed the opinion that before staff officers at Groups, Commands and at the Air Ministry were allowed to dictate the techniques and methods of flying jet aircraft, they should be made to fly them and gain actual experience on them. A very valid point. There was a decidedly deathly hush as the young officer sat down. Everyone waited for the explosion – but it did not come! Instead, Basil Embry stood up stiffly with his hands thrust into his tunic side-pockets, as was his habit, and in his rather hard, sharp and very emphatic voice said – 'And by God they will!' Before a week had passed the very senior staff officers were descending upon us from above, including the Commander-in-Chief of Fighter Command, to be given training on jet aircraft. This was typical of Basil Embry, and one could clearly see why he had become so famous during the war. I was told later on by another C-in-C that it was this ruthless character in Embry that prevented him becoming the Chief of the Air Staff, or the head of NATO.

The de Havilland Chipmunk and the Percival Prentice

During 1947 we were given two new aeroplanes to assess for instructional purposes. The first one was the de Havilland Chipmunk, which had just been designed and built in Canada. The aircraft we had was the only one in the country and was civil registered G-AVVD. It was a very good aeroplane, as has been proved by its wide use since. The second aircraft was the Percival Prentice, which was an attempt at producing a new trainer which could be used both for elementary and advanced instruction. It had three seats, two side by side for the instructor and pupil, and an extra seat for another pupil to sit behind those in front to gain experience by watching what was going on. It also had full radio and equipment for standard beam approach (SBA). In contrast to the Chipmunk, the Prentice was not a successful aeroplane. It was too heavy and cumbersome for the engine power and it was stodgy to fly, and it also 'glided like a brick'! Several modifications were made to it to improve its handling characteristics, such as turning up the wingtips and increasing the keel surface at the tail end.

Ken Tapper and I took it up for spinning trials, which gave us a hair-raising time. We found that, once in a settled spin, often two hands were needed to get the control column forward sufficiently to get out of the spin, and on one occasion both of us had to use quite a lot of force to move the stick forward. When we landed we found that a handling pilot who was writing the pilot's notes for the Prentice had had a similar experience, and only recovered from his spin at about 500 feet.

When I rang Boscombe Down, the experimental establishment which had tested the aeroplane, to enquire what they had found in their tests, I was told that the 'stick force' in spin recovery was rather high (90 lb if I remember rightly)! Our conclusions were that one certainly could not expect a pupil on his first solo to recover satisfactorily from a spin in a Prentice! It was used for training, of course, after some necessary modifications.

A NEW CONCEPT IN LEARNING TO FLY

As we had been engaged for some time in pressing the idea of 'all-weather flying', that is, to teach pilots to accept flying in conditions of bad weather and at night as quite normal, we did a very successful experiment to support the idea.

In this experiment we used the Percival Prentice, because it was available and had full radio equipment, and we taught one of our navigators to fly. Almost all the dual instruction was given in bad weather conditions, when close radio control was essential, and the chap did his first solo flight in quite thick weather, almost fog – using his radio aids and the standard beam approach. Standing on the tarmac and watching this first solo, we were unable to see the Prentice from the time he took off and climbed up off the runway until he returned and was within 100 feet of touchdown.

ECFS was well known for its out-of-the-ordinary ideas, and a number of experiments were done, especially during the war, mainly to find quicker methods of instruction. One was to teach pupils to fly by giving them a beam approach course to see if they could absorb the basic flying techniques while learning a specialist technique. Another was to see if the advanced flying training phase could be cut out by putting pupils straight from the Magister and their elementary instruction onto operational aircraft.

Prior to and during the early days of the Second World War the aim of the flying training was to fly the aeroplane safely and well. The performance of aircraft, engines and equipment was limited, and accordingly so were the pilot's capabilities. Few pilots had experienced operating in severe weather conditions, on top of which the added distraction and effects of enemy action could be dangerous and perhaps fatal. There had been little or no attempt to train aircrew in bad weather, or in the event of engine failure on multi-engined aircraft. There was certainly very little emphasis on the need for the pilot to be trained to fly his aircraft to the limit of its capability, and to cope with the circumstances when he took it beyond these limits.

From the early days of the war and throughout its duration ECFS continually stressed the need to train for 'all-weather' conditions and to fly the aeroplane to its limit – in fact to get into difficulties, to experience them and overcome them.

Our students were encouraged to 'look' for bad weather such as cu-nimbs (thunderstorms) and frontal conditions and fly through them – to learn to trust their instruments and aids and to fly in cloud and bad visibility as much as possible.

They were also taught to fly their multi-engined aircraft on asymmetric power – by 'failing' one engine on a turn, even two and three engines on a four-engined aircraft – failing the engines at critical times such as on take-off and when approaching to land, and getting pilots thoroughly familiar with these conditions and the capabilities and the limits of the aircraft. This was good training when simulating an engine failure at a critical phase. In all these cases the engines failed were actually stopped and not just throttled back – to be used if need be!

By 1946 ECFS had logged well over 4,000 landings on asymmetric power. Even landings after normal training flights tended to be done with one or more engines switched off. There is no doubt that this philosophy put over by ECFS was instrumental in saving many lives and aircraft on operations and has contributed to the present-day all-weather capability of the RAF. Such training procedures increased the skills of the pilots and enabled them to deal with emergencies effectively and safely.

In the course of this kind of training some difficult, if not desperate, moments are bound to occur. One was where a Lancaster had been chasing thunderstorms round England and Scotland, at the same time dropping-off chaps at various airfields for their Easter break. Coming south from Prestwick, it tried to land at Shawbury in thick weather which was rapidly deteriorating. After three abortive attempts the pilot came back to Hullavington, which was just about as bad. Lyneham, the transport airfield nearby, had stopped flying, so Hullavington had to accept the Lancaster, which had not enough fuel to go elsewhere.

Visibility was less than 200 yards, and the only aid we had was standard beam approach – which was not a landing device. Also, the wind was at least 10 knots in completely the wrong direction, so that if the approach was made using the SBA the landing would have to made downwind and on a relatively short runway too. So the pilot, an experienced Liberator pilot, chose to ignore the SBA and approach into wind. But, in spite of hearing the main marker of the SBA which was just off the end of the runway, and the fact that we had lit a number of magnesium flares, he could not see the runway soon enough to land. After two attempts he decided to use the SBA and get the approach right and risk landing downwind, again with the help of the magnesium flares. Although we could not see the Lancaster, we were relieved to hear him on what seemed to be a good approach, and then we heard the crackle of the Merlin exhaust as he slammed the throttles closed – a short moment of silence and then the sharp squeal of the tyres on the runway told us that he was on the ground. Only as the Lancaster slowed to a halt near the end of the runway could we see its dim shape in the fog for the first time.

On another occasion, this time in heavy cloud down to a few hundred feet and rain, we were doing an intensive SBA exercise with some seven or eight aircraft in order to try out a stacking and holding procedure, followed by the aircraft landing in quick succession. This technique was developed into the system used by most civil airports today. In this exercise I was flying an Oxford and was given a height to hold above the beam at about 7,000 feet. All went well until I had reached the allotted height and began to follow the figure-of-eight pattern – then the beam equipment in the aircraft failed, and immediately after I had reported this fact the RT failed, too! My passenger was not experienced in the Oxford or the equipment, although he was a pilot. Our efforts to get the equipment going again failed, so I decided to fly north-east away from the airfield and all the other aircraft and descend carefully in an area which I knew to be clear of exceptionally high ground. This plan succeeded, and we broke cloud at about 200 feet in the Cirencester area, from where I easily made my way back to Hullavington at low level.

A MYSTERY VISITOR

One afternoon when we were not flying we noticed a Miles Master III make a circuit of the airfield and land, but there had been no call on the radio from it. The plane taxied round the perimeter track towards the hangars and control tower, but instead of parking as we expected it went straight past and went to the take-off point, took off and after completing a circuit landed again, but still no radio call. This performance was repeated twice more, and then when the plane was passing the hangars for the third time we went out and stopped it. We asked the pilot if he was having trouble with his radio. 'No', he said. We asked who he was talking to. 'Lyneham Tower', he replied. He was actually asking Lyneham (some ten miles away) for his landing, take-off and taxiing instructions, and they were giving them – but he was at Hullavington. This was quite incredible, especially as Lyneham didn't appear to appreciate that he wasn't at Lyneham!

In those war and post-war days it was quite easy to pick the wrong airfield because there were so many of them and they were often very close together – also they usually looked much alike.

CHAPTER 16

Goodbye to Flying Training

It was now 1948 and there were signs that the peacetime shape of the RAF was being formed. I had been transferred, on paper, to the Aircraft Control Branch which was being formed at that time, but I was told that I was to be retained in the Flying Training Command for EFS duties. This situation was a little confusing. If a choice had been available I would have preferred to remain in flying training.

In due course, on 5 April 1948, I was posted to Fighter Command and to RAF Neatishead (near Norwich) for duties as a fighter controller. So began some eleven and a half years of working underground in artificially lit and ventilated operations rooms. All these operations rooms were somewhat remote from our living and administration quarters, and in most cases travel to and from work meant rather tiring coach journeys at all hours of the day and night – since the work was essentially watch keeping.

FIGHTER CONTROL, 5 APRIL 1948

The work of fighter control comprised two associate roles: firstly that of reporting all movements of aircraft as seen by radar and identifying them as friend or foe, and secondly in response to that information controlling the fighters in the area against the enemy. Naturally, as the foe did not exist in peacetime, exercises were continually being arranged to provide the enemy either as pairs of fighters practising interceptions against one another or in more complicated exercises using bombers, and eventually NATO aircraft. The reporting role went on day and night twenty-four hours per day and seven days a week, while the control role was rather less continuous, usually from 8 a.m. to 5 p.m., and then at night whenever the night-fighters were flying. We also had a role in training the auxiliary fighter control units which were the territorial reserves in the event of war. These units worked with us during most weekends and occasionally one evening each week.

THE AIR FORCE CROSS

Nearly four years after I was told I had been awarded the Air Force Cross, it finally arrived. It was while on duty as chief controller at Neatishead that I received my AFC, a most un-ceremonious occasion. The clerk in the orderly room came into the control cabin, gave me a registered parcel and simply said, 'Sign here, please, Sir!'

There was no citation with the medal explaining the reason for the award, and I had to wait a further three years for this document. When it finally arrived the citation read as follows:

> This officer is Chief Flying Instructor of CFS and has done excellent work as a flying instructor over a period of four years, which have followed a tour of operational flying. He devotes almost the whole of his time to his work and has few other interests. He is exceptionally enthusiastic and hard-working and has contributed in large measure to the improvement in training standards in this colony. He has made himself an acknowledged expert on flying instruction by study and practice.

Within three months I was to go to Germany to take over a mobile radar control and reporting unit at Handorf, Münster, with the rank of squadron leader.

CHAPTER SEVENTEEN

Germany

The air trip to Wünsdorf from Northolt was in a cold and un-comfortable Dakota. The weather was poor and the very bumpy flight made the crude canvas seating of this sparsely fitted wartime troop carrier even less enjoyable. After going to the HQ of British Air Forces of Occupation (BAFO) to book in – this was at Bad Eilsen – I went on to HQ No. 2 Group at Sundern.

HANDORF

Twelve kilometres east of Münster and about thirty west of Gütersloh, Handorf was a small village. There was a German airfield nearby, completely devastated, buildings largely wrecked and runways entirely broken up. The radar and supporting vehicles were sited in the middle of the airfield on the intersection of the runways. We had a Nissen-type hut for the technical staff and stores.

The radar vehicles were Type 13 (height finders), Type 14 (plan positive low coverage) and Type 15 (medium and high cover plan positive), all on Canadian Mack chassis. The control vehicle was a large AEC Matador. The electricity supply was from mobile diesel generator on an Austin chassis, one for each operational vehicle and one for the two radio transmitters and receivers, which were also separate vehicles on Austin chassis. There was a workshop vehicle and several water carriers and the usual load carriers – quite a complex, which had to be spread out to the end of long cables from each other to minimise interference.

Domestically and administratively the unit was known by the title No. 15054 Fighter Director Post, and had been used throughout the advance into Europe and also during the Berlin Airlift. The unit was housed in a large hotel in the village of Handorf which went under the name of the Boniburg.

MOBILITY

Being a mobile operational unit, one of the obvious priorities was to ensure that we were actually capable of being mobile. This became abundantly clear when one studied the political situation between east and west. At this time there were some 700 refugees coming over the border each week, and incidents both on the ground and in the air were common.

The tension between east and west was such that the whole of BAOR and BAFO had to be very much on the alert, and literally be ready for anything. September was said to be the trickiest month, for it was thought a war would most likely start then, when the harvests had been got in!

In the event of a full mobilisation, the families posed a big problem, for one of the first moves would be to evacuate the hundreds of service families. Highly secret plans abounded, and of course my unit was involved in these. The Army must have remembered the September idea, for during that month in my first year at Handorf, when I was ill in bed, they rang me, and when I answered the phone all I heard was the word 'Barker'. 'Barker' was one of the evacuation plan codewords! I said I had an SNCO as duty officer at the Boniburg, and that he could deal with the situation. 'No, he couldn't.' I would have to go. I had to wrap up, get the car out and go to the Boniburg, where I got the plan out of the safe to see what 'Barker' meant. I had to acknowledge this word by giving back the appropriate codeword reply. I was greatly relieved to find that this 'lark' I was on was just a test of communications, and not the order to put the evacuation plan into operation – thank goodness!

However, I had to make sure that the whole unit, airmen, vehicles and families were capable of being moved out and evacuated at a moment's notice. We had some thirty vehicles in all, but drivers for only about ten or so. We would not be able to use the German civilians so we had to train our radar operators and plotters to drive. This we did mainly in off-duty periods, and with excellent co-operation from all involved we had ample qualified and licensed drivers within three months. In the mean-time all vehicles were given a thorough check. This was particularly important, for fifteen or so operational vehicles didn't appear to have been moved from their sites for a very long time. The next job was to arrange an exercise to practise getting on the move, and then resiting to become operational again. We incorporated a convoy trip of twenty miles in this test to check the road-worthiness of the vehicles and to give the drivers road experience on their allotted vehicles. It was a great success, with only one minor breakdown. It gave us all, and particularly the newly trained drivers, much confidence.

My final task in the evacuation problem was to choose suitable routes into Holland which could take our very large and heavy vehicles. Some were over fifteen feet high, and there were many low bridges and also some that wouldn't be strong enough to take their weight safely.

DISCIPLINE AND COURTS MARTIAL

I had only one real troublemaker at Handorf: he was repeatedly absent without leave (AWOL). With no legitimate excuse he obviously had to be punished, and each time his sentences of confined to camp (CC) had to be heavier and heavier, with no sign of him turning over a new leaf. Because his absence meant absence from duty, forfeiture of pay for the period of absence was mandatory, but no doubt for reasons known only to the airman this loss of pay was no deterrent, and even when the award of 28 days' CC was reached there seemed to be no improvement. Now, because of the automatic stopping of pay I always had to ask the chap, after I had decided he was guilty, if he would accept my punishment or if he wished to be tried by court martial – which was his right if he so wished. Then, as I had reached the limit of my punishment in CC and could only resort to detention, and this could not easily be carried out at Handorf, I was deter-mined to shake him if he came before me again for absence.

I didn't have to wait very long, and when I put the usual question to him he eagerly chose to accept my punishment. Then came the bombshell: I told him that I would decline to pass sentence but would send him to be court-martialled. He was dealt with by court martial (CM) at Gütersloh and taken to the UK to serve his detention in the 'glasshouse'.

At Gütersloh there was trouble of a more serious kind. Some RAF Regiment chaps were getting out of hand, and finally several were court-martialled for beating up a German at a local dance hall – the German died. This court martial was held by UK officers, and attracted a lot of publicity in the British press. The sentences were of long imprisonment. No doubt the discipline at Gütersloh was lax, for very soon the CO was replaced by Group Captain Dudley Lewis, a well-known disciplinarian who was our sector commander at Horsham St Faith (in Neatishead days). His instructions were obviously to 'clean up' the station – which he did in no uncertain fashion. First reports from Gütersloh were that he was 'terrible' and holding very tough parades. However, within six months he was thought to be a wonderful CO. I have always thought that a station with a strict, but fair, discipline was invariably a happy one, but that an 'easy' one was often an unhappy one sooner or later.

GERMAN TELEVISION

Towards the end of my stay in Germany television was set up, and one of the first stations to start broadcasting was at Düsseldorf. Although we were quite some distance away, it completely blotted out our radar display when our aerial was looking towards the television station – by international agreement the German television had been allocated the exact frequency on which our radar operated! Our complaints and protests were of no avail!

CHAPTER 18

Home Again

Early in December 1952 I was informed that my relief, Sqn Ldr Ted Lacey, would be arriving from the UK shortly, so it seemed that I would be home for Christmas. Going back by car and boat, Elsie and John would be with me.

I had met Ted Lacey before briefly and knew him to be ex-aircrew, an engineer on Stirling bombers. He was awarded the DSO for an outstanding effort in bringing his Stirling back from a bombing raid on Germany after his pilot had been killed. Although not a pilot, he obviously knew enough, as an engineer, to take over and fly back and get it down safely. Quite a remarkable achievement.

So, with the unit handed over, we packed the car with our belongings and set off for Holland and the Hook port. I don't think there was one cubic inch of space left unoccupied in the car. Cars did not drive onto the ships as they do now. Each one had to be lifted by crane into the hold of the ship. The journey was quite uneventful, although the sea crossing was a bit upsetting.

Getting through customs at Harwich was easy; the AA man was most helpful, and the only question asked by the customs officer was whether I had got anything except personal belongings and the usual gifts for the family. Not so easy was the clearance of the Army officer behind me in the queue. When asked whether he had got anything to declare he said he had only got his gun – the reaction was to inspect his vehicle and contents very thoroughly.

Before I left Germany Ted Lacey had hinted that my new unit would be Sopley, a new master radar station near Christchurch. I had to report to HQ No. 11 Group the day after arriving in the UK, so having taken Elsie and John to Eaton Lodge I went to Uxbridge.

Yes, it was Sopley, and they wanted me to be there as soon as possible. Naturally I wanted to take the disembarkation leave which was due to me, and after some discussion we settled on a fortnight. Of course we went north to Darlington, where I left the family, and then reported to Sopley.

SOPLEY – NO. 469 SIGNALS UNIT

Having arrived at Sopley (near Christchurch), I found that the living and administration accommodation was newly built of temporary hutting in the favourite pheasant covert of Lord Manners, close to Bransgore. Previously the unit had been housed at the wartime airfield of Ibsley, near Ringwood. The reason for the choice of this new site was to use the some 120 oak trees for natural camouflage against air attack. The operations site was a couple of miles to the west, near the village of Sopley, and was the old wartime radar operations room, which was badly out of date. A new operations room and modern equipment was due to be built alongside, but this time deeply underground to withstand air attack. The digging of this 'hole', some thirty to forty feet down and providing three storeys of operational and engineering facilities, had already been done, and the majority of the building was completed. The radar and signals equipment was being installed – the whole thing was reputed to be costing at least three million pounds.

There were no married quarters, and apart from a few hirings all married men were either living in camp or were in private accommodation.

PROMOTION

The rank of the CO post at Sopley was squadron leader, but as the role of the unit was upgraded from that of a ground-controlled interception unit (GCIU) to that of a master radar station (MRS), it was to be commanded by a wing commander. So, soon after taking over I was promoted. With this increase in rank, of course, came greater responsibility. A bigger and more important station and operational role, with much more and modern radar and signals equipment, meant more personnel – in fact a total of some 800 all ranks, of whom thirty-three were officers – some change from Handorf!

A lone Heinkel III K being chased by a pilot of 41 Squadron. This was the type shot down on 17th October 1939. Picture signed by "Cowboy" Blatchford and E Shipman and dated 17th October 1939. [RAF Crown Copyright]

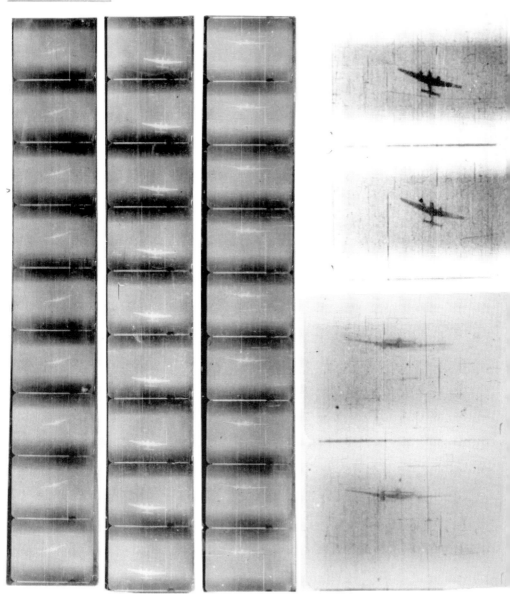

CAMERA GUN FILM OF DESTRUCTION OF GERMAN
ME 110D OF 1/ZG 76 BASED AT STAVANGER BY A
SPITFIRE OF N° 41 SQUADRON BASED AT CATTERICK

DATE: 15 AUG 1940   TIME: 1336   PLACE: 3 MILES EAST OF BARNARD
                                                                    CASTLE
GERMAN CREW: OBER LIEUTENANT KETLING & 1 CREW

RAID CONSISTED OF: 34 ME 110's   65 HE 111's   (OBGEFREITER VOLK)

DESTROYED :   7 ME 110's   8 HE 111's

N° 41 SQN. SCORE: 7 CONFIRMED & 7 PROBABLES

R.A.F. LOSSES: NIL

Cine Camera gun film exposures of Hans Kettling's Me110 being attacked from astern by PO
"Shippy" Shipman, Frames on the right – range estimated at 200 yards. Lower right picture show
smoke emitting from starboard (right) engine. *[EA Shipman Crown copyright]*

R.A.F. Form 1151.

COMBAT REPORT.

Sector Serial No. .... (A)

Serial No. of Order detailing Flight or Squadron to
Patrol .... (B) SPITFIRE K9805

Date .... (C) 14.10.39.

Flight, Squadron .... (D) Flight: B Sqdn.: 41

Number of Enemy Aircraft .... (E) One

Type of Enemy Aircraft .... (F) HE 111

Time Attack was delivered .... (G) 1025

Place Attack was delivered .... (H) 20 miles NE WHITBY

Height of Enemy .... (J) 0 - 1,000'

Enemy Casualties .... (K) 1 A/c 1ERSOWED U/R

Our Casualties .... Aircraft .... (L) NIL.

.... Personnel .... (M) NIL.

GENERAL REPORT .... (R)

E A evaded by accelerating & diving to gain
speed. Upper rear gunner returned fire from amidships
turret using tracer ammunition — No apparent effect.

Light Blue Grey on under surface & large black crosses
on white background mid way between fuselage &
wing tips. No other colouring observed.

After third burst of fire engines smoked heavily
a/c continued its shallow dive & landed on the water.
Two occupants climbed out, one appeared to be wounded
as he was helped back into the cockpit.

Opened fire at 450-500 yds, closed to fire at 200-250.

Closed too rapidly - possibly due to EA's engine packing up.
Rear gunner ceased to fire after 2nd or 3rd burst.

Appox amount of ammunition
expended - 2,200 to
2,400

Signature Brotherman F/S.

Section GREEN
Flight 'B'
Squadron Squadron No. 41

Informed by H/q rebel Destroyer picking up survivors.
Later informed that survivors had been picked up.
Still later. Not picked up. — Drifted ashore appox 40 hours
after combat, in rubber boat. — Came ashore at Sandsend - taken prisoner by
special constable.

Copy of the original Combat report written after the encounter.

Pilot Officer Eric "Lockie" Lock (Red 3) scored his first victory when he hit both engines of an Me110 which later crashed into Seaham Harbour.

Hans Kettling's wings badge from his breas pocket of his Luftwaffe uniform and given t "Shippy" Shipman in 1980. [J Shipman]

Hans –Ulrich Kettling, 1/ZG 76 at Trondheim Norway August 1940. [H Kettlin

Hans Kettling's ME Bf 110 D-/R-1 Wk Nr. 3155 (M8 + CH) being prepared prior to 15th August 1940 to accept a belly fuel tank, or "dachshund belly " for the long crossing of the North Sea from Norway to North England, and hopefully the return journey. [H Kettling]

Luftwaffe ground crew arm the two machine guns mounted in the nose of Hans Kettling's ME Bf 110. [H Kettling]

Hans Kettling's ME Bf 110 before the attack on England. Note the belly fuel tank. [H Kettling]

Hans Kettling's ME Bf 110. Running up the engines before take off. No belly fuel tank fitted at this time. *[H Kettling]*

Ground crew relaxing before Hans Kettling departs for England. *[H Kettling]*

The result of the encounter between "Shippy" Shipman and Hans Kettling. The tail section of Hans Kettling's ME Bf 110 after crash landing in a field near to Barnard Castle. *[B Norman]*

The fuselage section of Hans Kettling's ME Bf 110 after crash landing and coming to rest against a telegraph pole in a field near to Barnard Castle. *[B Norman]*

The centre, wing, engines and cockpit section of Hans Kettling's ME Bf 110 after crash landing in a field near to Barnard Castle. *[B Norman]*

The search for the site of Han Kettling's forced landing at Broomielaw Farm on 18th June 1987 is complete. (from left to right) Hans Kettling, "Shippy" Shipman, Margaret Kettling, Mollie Shipman, Amy Shipman, Gerri Shipman. *[J Shipman]*

"Shippy" Shipman (left) with Hans Kettling standing on the crash site at Broomielaw Farm, Barnard Castle on 18th June 1987. Compare the background in the picture here with the earlier one of the crashed aircraft. *[J Shipman]*

Hans Kettling (left) and Ted "Shippy" Shipman meet once again in 1990 to be interviewed for a Newspaper article. *[Times Newspapers Lt*

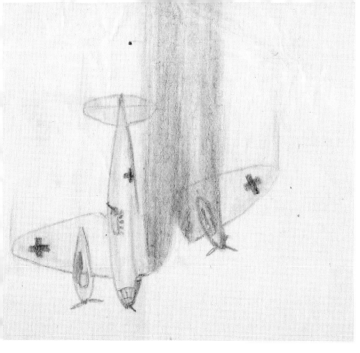

Sketch drawn by "Shippy" Shipman after returning to base to show the underside of the Heinkel and the port wing breaking off before impacting the water. *[EA Shipman]*

Getting ready for an instructional flight. The pupil is in the rear cockpit and "Shippy" Shipman is giving some last minute instructions before taking his position in the front cockpit. The pilots communicate using a speaking or Gosport tube. Note the parachute which will fit in the bucket shaped seat. CFS Upavon 1941. Aircraft is a Miles Master III fitted with a Wasp engine. *[E A Shipman]*

Pre flight briefing at CFS Upavon 1941. Instructor on left is "Shippy" Shipman. Aircraft is a Miles Master III fitted with a Wasp engine. [E A Shipman]

Flg Off Olley the pilot on the left and Sqn Ldr Hunn holding a dead Rain Bird after it had struck the aerial of the Harvard during flight. [E A Shipman]

Empire Flying School 1946. A wide range of aircraft were available and a representative selection of aircraft used are shown: Back row left to right: Avro Lancaster, Bristol Buckmaster, NA Mitchell, Vickers Wellington, DH Mosquito. Front row left to right: Airspeed Oxford, Miles Master III, Harvard, Supermarine Spitfire IX, Supermarine Spitfire V, DH Tiger Moth, Airspeed Hotspur, German Bucker.

"Shippy" Shipman discussing the finer points of the jet engine in the Display Hall.

RAF Handorf 2TAF Germany HQ of 15054 FDP "The Boniburg ". 1950-52

Guests at the 1953 Officers' Mess Christmas Ball 1953. Left to Right: "Shippy" Shipman, Guest, Elsie Shipman, other guests.

The Goldsmith's Trophy for light machine gun won by a record score of 529/550 Left to Right: P/O Harry Reed-Purvis (Captain of team and RAF Regiment), "Shippy" Shipman, Flt Lt "Tich" Burton and Cpl Stewart.

Flt Lt. "Shippy" Shipman 1943.

Edward or as he preferred to be called Ted "Shippy" Shipman in the cockpit of a Panavia Tornado F3 fighter in November 1997 during an invitation from Flt Lt Greg Hurst to visit the Tri-National Tornado Training Establishment at RAF Cottesmore. Flt Lt Greg Hurst was a Tornado Pilot at RAF Cottesmore and was killed in a mid air collision between a Tornado on a low level training flight and a light aeroplane over Derbyshire. On 4th September 1998 "Shippy" was remembered with a period of silence at a Wings parade at the Royal Air Force College, Cranwell when the graduating aircrew received their flying badges. *[Picture by kind permission of RAF Cottesmore. Crown copyright].*

The bravery and skill of men such as Bader, Lock and Malan for the RAF or Galland, Mölder and Wick of the Luftwaffe, were drawn in contrail lines of the utmost clarity. But not all could be aces. Up there were also the average – men like Ted "Shippy" Shipman, son of a Leicestershire farmer, and Hans Kettling, son of a Dusseldorf engraver. They said that not for one moment did they feel heroic; much less did they see themselves as invincible. *[Times Newspapers Ltd]*

Following my promotion, the operations officer was to be a squadron leader. But 'Tealeaf' Holmes, as he was known, was not to be the one. Although he was an efficient and well-known fighter controller, he lacked responsibility in some ways, and was inclined to do things which upset the 'applecart'. A horsy man, he was known to bring his horse into the officers' mess on a Sunday morning when out for a ride. He was also involved in some kind of incident with a more senior officer on another station which I had to smooth out on my arrival. Anyway, he was sent to another job, and four years later I met him again, this time in Cyprus as a squadron leader.

THE 'HOLE'

The old operations room, built early in the war, was a small affair above ground with blast-proof walls around it. It was a small plotting room about thirty-six feet square, with three small over-looking cabins for the sector controller, the chief controller and the liaison officers. Behind these were three, even smaller, inter-ception cabins where interceptions were controlled from radar display. Below these cabins were the technical staff and their equipment which fed the control radar displays above.

The new operations room (correctly named the R3 underground GCI technical building), or the 'hole', as it became universally known, was a vastly different affair. First of all it was totally below ground, and it was a very large building of three storeys. There was very much more radar of the latest kind and with about three times the control capacity. The communications facilities, radio, inter-communication between the controllers and their teams and with other stations, HQ Fighter Command operation room and airfields were greatly improved. The GPO was responsible for all landlines and telephones, and for that purpose provided an engineer on permanent duty. When all the MRSs were built and working – there were only five, as opposed to some ten or twelve GCIUs previously, it was said that the Fighter Command control and reporting defence system occupied a quarter of the GPO telephone lines in the country!

The R3 was never intended to survive a direct hit from a nuclear weapon but was designed to withstand a near-miss from Russian pattern bombing with 2,200 lb armour-piercing high-explosive bombs (BRAB) dropped from 35,000 feet.

To ensure an adequate and continuous electricity supply we had an automatic standby generator on the domestic site which started up the moment any failure in the grid supply occurred. Sometimes when the mains supply was unsteady or low we would go onto standby to get a satisfactory radar picture. The GPO was equally particular, for it had its own rectification plant and also standby batteries.

The radar had quite a 'Rolls-Royce' character compared with our old equipment. It could look further, nearly twice as far, and its accuracy and definition were very much greater. From the operator's and controller's point of view the displays were larger, clearer and extremely flexible in adjustment for range and scale. The tubes were of a 'daylight' type, and we didn't need to sit in almost complete darkness to see the echoes. There was much less eye strain.

The new station became operational in the summer of 1954, using the call-sign 'AVO'; it was fitted with the following radars: one Type 7 Mk II, one Type 11 (Mobile) Mk VII, two Type 13 Mk VI, two Type 13 Mk VII, one Type 14 Mk 8 and one Type 14 Mk 9. A new domestic camp for 450 personnel was built near Bransgore village, but until this was complete accommodation was provided until 1952 at RAF Ibsley, which had closed as an active base in 1946.[1]

The living conditions in the 'hole', apart from being constantly lit by fluorescent lights and having a sometimes rather noisy air-conditioning system playing a steady background accompaniment to our existence, were very good. There were offices, rest rooms, a canteen and of course toilets. The latter, being some considerable depth below ground level, posed a special problem, but the device to pump out the sewage seemed to work well. On the other hand, with a very high water table in the surrounding land, we were close to the river Avon, and we were unable to prevent water seeping in; the pressure on the shell of the building must have been considerable. Anyway, a simple solution was found by putting a sump in the floor of the bottom storey and fitting an electric pump controlled by a float-operated switch. This pumped out the water as it collected.

SECURITY

The 'hole' and its radar aerials above were a major security risk. Everything was 'secret', and everyone had to have a special pass to enter. The whole area was surrounded by stout chain-link fencing about eight feet high, with ample barbed wire above. The gates were always locked unless opened by the military police for someone to enter or leave. A bell-push on the gate rang through to the guardroom, the only building on the site, and designed to look rather like a small bungalow. In the 'bungalow' (some say it was supposed to look like a golf club pavilion) was a strong wire grille, beyond which one could not go until the visitor's pass had been verified under an ultra-violet lamp to indicate the right to enter. This right could be for a single station only, or a group of them or all in the Command, but this information was invisible unless seen under UV lighting. In addition, armed RAF police, police dogs and their handlers were always on duty.

But this was not all. There were frequent and unexpected tests of security by all sorts of methods and ruses. Individuals would try to get in with faulty or incorrect passes, either as civilians from the radar firms or as visiting serving officers from Group, Command or the Air Ministry. One rather rotten trick, we thought, was a woman rattling the gate of a remote VHF site at night. She was dishevelled and appeared to have blood on her face. She said her husband had been hurt in a car accident on the road nearby – could she have a drink of water and telephone for assistance? She turned out to be a service policewoman testing the security arrangements!

On another occasion, this time at the 'hole' and during a bank holiday weekend, two civilians arrived with some technical equipment and genuine documents to support the equipment, but with forged passes. Unfortunately, the young policeman, his second time on duty alone, failed to detect the forgeries and let the men in, after which they produced their real identities – Criminal Investigation Branch Police NCOs. Even the Commander-in-Chief Fighter Command, Air Marshal Sir Basil Embry, had to show his pass, and he expected to have to do so.

One very interesting visit I made was to Boscombe Down, the aircraft-testing station. This was to discuss with the group captain in charge of flying arrangements for us to control the Boscombe experimental aircraft in flights which exceeded the speed of sound in order to avoid damage by the sonic booms to private property, and to Salisbury cathedral in particular. We had already been controlling Neville Duke, the Hawker test pilot, on similar flights. Also, we had been involved in daily test flights by a Canberra from Bristol with Olympus engines climbing to 60,000 feet.

While at Boscombe Down on this visit I was fortunate enough to see Wg Cdr Roland Beamont make the second flight in the prototype PI (Lightning) – quite a thrilling sight.

Another visit worth recounting was a mysterious Wg Cdr Acott. One day Fighter Command rang up to say that Acott would ring me for an appointment and I was to give him full co-operation. Eventually he did ring and booked a day for his visit; however, he declined to indicate his business. Later, when I had to contact him by telephone, I had a great deal of difficulty in getting through to him. His telephone extension number was ex-directory and they didn't know of him.

When he arrived at Sopley we had to talk quite alone and undisturbed, since the nature of this work turned out to be 'TOP SECRET'. At certain times and on certain dates he wanted our operators to look for unusual echoes coming in from the sea. The trouble was that neither the controllers, supervisors nor the radar operators were allowed to be told what we were to look for, or what was involved! We never saw anything which we could positively identify, and as Acott went away happy I suppose that whatever he was concerned with was a success, since it was not seen on the radar – to us a mystery unsolved! Was this a trial of 'stealth' technology?

SHOOTING AT BISLEY

Being interested in shooting and having a very keen young RAF Regiment officer, Harry Reed-Purvis, I did all I could to get something going, with the idea of going to Bisley once again. Knowing the difficulty of getting rifles good enough for competition shooting, together with the opportunity to practise enough to put up a good show, we decided to go for the Light Machine-Gun Trophy presented by the Goldsmiths' Company. This competition needed only three in the team and one bren-gun.

It was a complicated exercise, which involved the team running down from 600 yards to 100 yards, firing a given number of rounds at 600, 500, 400, 300, 200, and 100 yards – all to be done against the clock and running each hundred yards and firing the necessary rounds during the timed appearance of the target. Each member of the team took turns in carrying the bren-gun and firing it. I was sure that careful preparation and training against a stopwatch was a most important factor, and Reed-Purvis thoroughly agreed. Having done a good few 'rundowns' with a rifle, I knew that one tended to run too fast, so that one became more exhausted and out of breath than was necessary, making accurate shooting less likely.

Carrying my ideas further, I insisted that the team should be uniformly dressed in battle dress, gaiters and boots, rather than let them wear what they liked. I also insisted that they should run in a disciplined fashion by keeping in step with one another. I thought this would not only create a good impression but would help in their timing on the run between each 100-yard distance. All this I reckoned would produce a competent and a confident team, giving them the best possible chance to shoot well. The stopwatch became a permanent part of their kit throughout and in the actual competition. All members of the team, including the reserve, were most enthusiastic, and we all felt they would do well.

The great day at Bisley came, and we found that we were on the first detail. This suited the team since we were keen to get the job done and finished. Wishing the team good luck I watched them get on to the 600-yard firing-point all neatly turned out and in great contrast to some of the other teams. But I thought, perhaps looks are not everything, and maybe we would be beaten on the shooting.

When the targets at the butts appeared for their short period the first volley was fired, and immediately off the chaps went to the next marker. Immediately I could see the value of the disciplined and strictly timed training. Their running was unhurried and delightful to watch. Then I began to wonder if they were too slow and might not get all their rounds off before the target disappeared. I anxiously waited for the volley of shots at each marker – all was well, for almost immediately the last round was fired the target disappeared. All went well and we now had to wait for the scores to come through.

The team arriving back at the detail tent just couldn't bear waiting for the results to be phoned through from the butts, but went for a walk. I waited with Reed-Purvis, and it seemed a long time though it was only a very few minutes. Then the announcement: Sopley 529 (out of 550)!

It was a record score, beating the previous best of 524. So we had done it. A remark from a member of another team made me smile: 'Where the hell is Sopley?' We had put Sopley well and truly on the map and we were all very happy. In 1976 Harry Reed-Purvis was an air commodore and Director of Ground Defence. He retired in 1982 as AVM Commandant-General of the RAF Regiment.

POSTING TO HQ NORTHERN SECTOR

By November 1955 I had been at Sopley nearly three years, and I was not surprised when I was warned for posting. This time it was to Headquarters Northern Sector at Shipton, just north of York, as Wing Commander Control and Reporting Staff Officer. Here at Shipton all our offices were underground and part of the sector operations centre; and our area of responsibility stretched from the Humber to the Scottish border, covering the reporting and control stations at Seaton Snook, Goldsborough, Bempton, Boulmer and Patrington.

All Shipton personnel were living at Linton-on-Ouse, but as there wasn't a married quarter available for me at the time I had to leave the family at Sopley while I went north to my new job and found private accommodation.

SHIPTON AND LINTON-ON-OUSE

On arrival at Linton I had to live in the mess until I could get accommodation for Elsie and John. I found that the Station Commander was Gp Capt Dennis Spotswood, who had been the CO at Coltishall when I was at Neatishead. Shipton personnel were all living at Linton and travelling to and fro daily by bus and car. The Sector Commander was an air commodore, three of us wing commanders, two for air matters and myself as the specialist staff officer for control and reporting. Our airfields were Linton, Leconfield, Driffield, and Church Fenton. Our staff were a Squadron Leader C & R as my deputy and another looking after signals and communications; then there was a civilian from the Home Office who was responsible for air raid warnings. On the control and reporting side we had some six radar stations – Seaton Snook (near Middlesbrough), Danby (Cleveland Hills), Goldsborough (Whitley), Bempton (Scarborough), Staxton (Filey) and Patrington (Spurn Head). As staff officers we had to pay regular visits to these stations and the airfields. Two of my Neatishead chums were at Patrington – Wg Cdr Joe Rye and Sqn Ldr Jim Watt – and the CO of one of the Driffield squadrons was a student of mine while at CFS Upavon – Wg Cdr Watt. One of our air staff officers was a student in my flight at Upavon, Wg Cdr McMillan, then a flight lieutenant.

NOTE

1. Nick Catford.

CHAPTER 19

Suez and Cyprus

The year was 1956, and by July it became obvious that trouble was brewing in the Middle East over the Suez Canal, which the Egyptians had grabbed and closed to all traffic. There were rumours that we might be involved in some sort of military action with the Israelis and the French. None of us at Shipton and Linton thought that, whatever happened, we as individuals would be directly affected. However, by mid-August I was warned that I would have to fly out to Cyprus with two other wing commanders in the fighter control branch within forty-eight hours.

I found out later that before my name was picked there were two others chosen – 'Little Willie' Le Rougetel (Neatishead 1948–50), who managed to side-step the job, and another whose wife was very ill with cancer. The two who went with me were Les Holman and Barney Oldfield, both well known to me.

The news of my going to Cyprus at such short notice was a shock for Elsie and John, particularly as there was so much trouble with the terrorists. After a hectic two days of kitting-up and inoculations, etc., I joined the other two wing commanders at Hendon and we emplaned at Blackbush in the evening on a charter DC6.

By midnight we were at Malta for a wash and quick meal while the aircraft was refuelled. Then in the morning the dazzling sun and heat of the Mediterranean climate greeted us as we landed at Nicosia in time for breakfast in the RAF mess where we were to stay. Our batman was a rather aged Turkish Cypriot, and it soon became obvious what he thought of the Greeks. The ratio of Greeks to Turks on the island was about 5:3, the Turkish having to take the 'stick' from their Greek 'bosses'.

156

Going into the mess bar for a pre-lunch drink we were greeted with, 'What the hell are you doing here?' from the Commander-in-Chief Middle East – Air Marshal Sam Patch (AOC 11 Group when I was at Sopley – now Sir Hubert Patch). With him was another old chum, Sqn Ldr Black, his statistician, who was in charge of the Norwich Fighter Control Unit in my days at Neatishead. Anyway, we did not have to buy our drinks that day.

The AOC Cyprus was another acquaintance, Air Commodore 'Paddy' Crisham, who used to be AOC 12 Group at Newton, also in my Neatishead days. In Cyprus he was our immediate boss and was to see us later in the day. Our job was to review the reporting and control radar system of the island and advise on its efficiency and improvement. We were given a helicopter to visit the remote radar sites. Flying was essential, not only to save time, but to avoid attacks by terrorists on road journeys.

There were three sites, Cape Greco in the south-east, Cape Gata in the south and Nicosia, with a co-ordinating operations room also at Nicosia. As an operational defence system it was almost non-effective. Much of the radar did not work very well, partly due to lack of spares and lack of use in exercises. What lines of communication existed were inadequate and unreliable. The operations room could hardly be described as such. Of course, one must remember that the Middle East was never faced with the need to provide the type of defence system that we had to put up in the UK.

Our report and recommendations were of necessity critical and strongly worded, especially because of the increasingly tense situation. Then, having taken these first steps, we set about helping to put matters as right as possible with the facilities available. The Signals Corps of the Army was pressed to provide more landlines and radio links, and the radar units were urged to improve their serviceability. We then concentrated on improving the control and reporting procedures for the operations room and its display of information. Finally, we set up a liaison line with the High Commissioner's office in Nicosia City to enable air raid warnings to be issued. To my great surprise the chap at the Commissioner's office when I was on duty was John Webster, who lived next door to my cousin Jack Clayton at Leicester. Jack, who was the Assistant Chief Constable for the county, and I had met John Webster over the garden fence while staying with Jack.

The permanent staff at Nicosia seemed to be quite unaware that there was any kind of emergency facing us. I think one of the reasons for this was the fact that the whole of the Suez operation was being handled and mounted from the UK. The C-in-C, Sam Patch, was given no responsibility at all – in fact an air marshal was sent out from the UK to take charge.

TERRORISM

Throughout the whole of our three-month stay in Cyprus, terrorism posed a big problem, and hardly a day passed without some incident occurring. On arrival we were issued with pistols and ammunition which we carried at all times, and we slept with them under our pillows. Ambushes were the most common type of attack. Just before we arrived a Land Rover was attacked on a hairpin bend on the pass over the Kyrenia, and an SSAFA woman welfare worker was killed. Then, while we were there, a small convoy of RAF vehicles was attacked while carrying water and food to the unit at Cape Greco. Shotguns loaded with small metal cubes were used, and five airmen were either killed or seriously injured.

In other attacks, despicable ruses would be used. One airman, while on duty in a lonely-sited Direction-Finding hut on the Nicosia airfield, was asked for a glass of water from outside his locked door. Quite against his orders he opened the door and was immediately shot down. Many attacks were made on individual servicemen who lived out with their families in the suburbs of Nicosia, usually when waiting for buses or shopping, or travelling to and from work. Many civilians were killed, and especially police, who were on detachments from the UK forces.

Without doubt the situation was tense, and one was inclined to be trigger happy and to shoot first and ask questions afterwards. One such incident turned out to be amusing for 'Tealeaf' Holmes and his wife, who were having dinner one dark evening. The weather was hot and the window open, and there was a suspicious noise outside the window. 'Tealeaf' grabbed his pistol and fired two shots through the open window: immediately there was a sound of 'someone' crashing through the bushes in the garden, and then there was a loud heehaw and a donkey went galloping down the road!

The centre of Nicosia and what was known as 'Murder Mile' were out of bounds to all troops, but Sqn Ldr Black persuaded me to drive with him through the area just to see what it was like – a typical Middle-Eastern narrow street crowded with shops of all descriptions, and on the whole not very inviting under the circumstances.

THE BUILD-UP

Back at Nicosia the build-up of troops and aircraft was growing very rapidly. A Hunter squadron from our own airfield in the UK and a Canberra squadron arrived, together with their ground staff and equipment – others followed. The mess at Nicosia was literally bursting at the seams. Tents were sprouting on every spare piece of ground around and meals had to be taken in three and four sittings. In the end we three less operationally active wingcos, together with a few others, moved out to the Dome Hotel in Kyrenia (reputedly the best on the island).[1] We lived there in absolute luxury, still sleeping with our pistols under our pillows and listening to the occasional bomb going off in the town. The local police station was a frequent target.

We travelled to and fro by thirty-seater coach, which had difficulty in negotiating the hairpin bends on the mountain pass, just the place where we might meet trouble. The driver and one escort were armed with rifles – just to give us confidence, no doubt, but of course that was the rule.

THE SUEZ OPERATION

Few of us thought that Egypt would ever be attacked. In spite of the preparations, we assumed that it was all just a show of force. Our daily contacts with the AOC, 'Paddy' Crisham, and other staff officers, including Sqn Ldr Black, as the C-in-C's staff, all confirmed this opinion. But we knew that the French were also involved, and we suspected that they were rather an unknown quantity; they were getting ready on Tymbu airfield, mainly with troop-carrying aircraft for the parachutists and equipment. Even in the afternoon of the attack 'Paddy' C. confirmed his opinion that no attack would take place; then, about an hour later, he strode into the operations room, threw his cap down on the table and exclaimed, 'It's bloody well on!', and almost immediately we heard the RAF Canberra bombers starting up.

We knew that the RAF Hawker Hunters, even with long-range tanks, would be operating over Suez at their limit in range, but in the event the RT communications were the biggest drawback, for Nicosia could not maintain contact. In this situation it was amusing, but rather ironic, that the British air traffic controllers at Beirut airport were in touch with the Hunters and were offering assistance!

A QUICK RETURN HOME

The AOC could see no further reason for us three 'musketeers' staying in Cyprus, since we had done all we could to prepare and get an acceptable defence system going, so he signalled the Air Ministry for our return authority. Then, a few days later just after lunch, a phone message came through to the officers' mess that we could go home on the next available plane. We quickly packed and were cleared for departure after handing in our equipment and our arms. We were on the tarmac by four o'clock.

Almost minutes later we were on the way in another charter DC6. Soon after take-off many of the civilian passengers showed considerable signs of concern and were looking out of the windows: we had an escort of our own squadron of Hunter aircraft, and they were formatting quite close to us on either side. It was a much-appreciated gesture of saying cheerio to us, and perhaps thanks, too. I wonder if the civilian captain of the DC6 appreciated their presence as much as we did!

We landed at Southend just before six a.m., and after going through customs we went by bus to Hendon, where a clean-up and a really good breakfast did us good. It took a little time to get our railway warrants to our various destinations, and then it was Kings Cross and to York for me.

NOTE

1. This hotel has quite a lot of history associated with it. Lawrence Durrell (who was a brother of the better-known Gerald), the author (of the book *Bitter Lemons*, written about the problems between the English, Greeks and Turks in Cyprus) and schoolteacher, had links to this hotel.

CHAPTER 20

Boulmer

The following year, 1957, saw the start of another move for us, this time still further north, to Boulmer, in Northumberland. The master radar station at Boulmer, similar to the one I had at Sopley, was one of our northern sector stations and was to become what was, in fact, an experimental station to develop more modern techniques in reporting, plotting and control of aircraft. In the 1956 Signals Plan, Boulmer was designated as one of nine master radar stations. RAF Anstruther was a satellite of Boulmer. In April 1957 it became a comprehensive GCI station. In November 1957 RAF Boulmer became 13 Group Control Centre, responsible for the GCI stations at RAF Buchan in the north of Scotland, RAF Killard Point in Northern Ireland and limited commitments from RAF Patrington (Eastern Sector MRS). It also assumed the role of Sector Operations Centre from RAF Shipton, which closed. Under the 1958 Signals Plan, Boulmer was retained as the 13 Group Control Centre and Headquarters, a Comprehensive Station and Master Radar Station responsible for Buchan, Hackett (Benbecula) and Killard Point, and the CEW stations at Saxa Vord and Aird Uig. This plan was later abandoned in favour of the Linesman/ Mediator system, with three SOCs at Buchan, Boulmer and Neatishead. As part of the 1958 Plan, Boulmer was selected to be upgraded with the installation of new high-powered Type 84 surveillance radar mounted above an R17 modulator building. This increased the range of detection and was able to penetrate the latest Soviet jamming technology. The Type 84 was unable to establish height, so two HF200 height finders were also added.[1]

One of the wing commanders at Shipton and I were to move up to Boulmer as master controllers to work on the new system under a very keen, uninhibited officer, Gp Capt James Coward, who had lost a leg in the Battle of Britain.

We were now appreciating the experience of living in one of the most attractive areas of Britain, and we found Northumberland to possess landscape features of great variety, from safe open beaches and dangerous rocky bays, through open country to the Cheviots.

The work at Boulmer was quite interesting, since it was leading us towards the automatic control of fighters and aiming to speed up the plotting, reporting and display of information by eliminating the manual efforts of the operators. The automatic control of the fighter through a computer was a long way off, but visits to Malvern Radar Research Establishment gave us an indication of what was to be possible in the future. We were given a relatively free hand to experiment with the radars, displays and the plotting procedures. In the immediate future we were concerned with the problem of controlling many fighters against many targets, while being subject to electronic countermeasures. One method used was to use a large, horizontal tube display to enable four controllers to work on it together. The modern radar equipment was a great help.

On the communications side we were happier than ever before. We had direct lines to Oslo in Norway and to Kastrup in Denmark, with exchanged officers available at either end. We had a Norwegian officer permanently with us, and one of ours was at Oslo. The co-operation was excellent, with no difficulty in knowing what was going on across the North Sea. On one occasion we close-controlled an experimental aircraft, the Fairy Delta II, across to Norway and back.

We were also involved in controlling the P1 aircraft, the Lightning, as it became, and the experimental firing of its Firestreak missiles over the Acklington range. We picked it up on the radar soon after it took off from Warton in Lancashire, and directed it to Scarborough, where we had to turn it north and to guide it on a controlled countdown in order to allow its missiles, when fired, to fall in the range area off the Northumberland coast.

Other unusual tasks we had were concerned with the lifeboats and coastguards. Radar reflectors were being fitted to the boats, and our low-looking radar was used to assess the value of these devices. The coastguards were also interested in the value of our radar to them in emergency when answering distress calls. One of my jobs was to lecture them on the radar equipment and our operational capabilities; this was done at their headquarters at Tynemouth. I was also given responsibility for the training of many of the airmen at Boulmer, especially on operational duties of their trades. Then there was the Newcastle Fighter Control Unit to accommodate at weekends and the arrangement of flying programmes for their training. From time to time I had to visit their training centre at Longbenton, on the northern outskirts of Newcastle.

NOTE

1. Nick Catford.

CHAPTER 21

So to Retirement

By 1958 I knew that unless something unusual happened I would be leaving the RAF by the end of 1959, when I would be fifty years old. So we began thinking about the future, what I would do and where we would live. In the meantime I had asked the Air Ministry for confirmation of my retirement date, which as expected was 9 December 1959.

We settled on Bottesford as our future home, and after consulting the council surveyor at Melton we decided to build a house there. Here there were good road and rail communications, adequate shops and a new school, run by my cousin Laurie Dewey.

Back at Boulmer in May, Elsie woke up one morning with severe abdominal pains on the left side. The doctor came quickly and got her into Alnwick Infirmary. After about a week of treatment the trouble subsided and she came home. All seemed well, but about a month later she was called to Newcastle for an X-ray and tests. No results were announced, but after we had been on leave again in August there was another call for admission to Newcastle for further tests and an exploratory operation. On 6 September she was obviously very poorly and complaining of pain in her right side, which she said was getting worse. The doctor said Elsie had an inoperable cancer. I was absolutely shattered, and found it difficult to know what to do. The end came for Elsie the following evening. There was nothing to do but to go home again. The next morning I had to tell John, and he was very brave indeed and sensibly agreed with me to go to school as usual. We tried to carry on life at Boulmer as best we could in the normal way, and set to work to get my service affairs squared up and be ready to move out on 9 November, when I was due to start a month's retirement leave.

I left the RAF quietly, for Eaton Lodge, since there was no home to go to. There was no sign of progress at Bottesford with the new house, and it was 16 June 1961 before we moved in.

So ended twenty-nine years and eight months in the Royal Air Force.

Postscript

Born in 1909, the youngest son of a tenant farmer in Leicester-shire, Ted 'Shippy' Shipman was one of 'The Few' who flew with No. 41 Squadron in the Battle of Britain. He left his father's farm in 1930 and enlisted in the RAF as an AC2 (driver, petrol). He flew for thirteen years of his thirty years' service, flew nearly forty different types of aircraft and achieved the highest grade of a flying instructor, and retired as a wing commander, decorated with the Air Force Cross, in December 1944.

His initial career took him through aero-engineering activities. After learning to fly during an annual leave, he eventually managed to secure a post with flying duties. Later he served with No. 41 Fighter Squadron 1936–40; No. 8 Service Flying Training School, Montrose, and Central Flying School, Upavon, in 1940; Flying Instructor's School at Empire Central Flying School, Hullavington, in 1942 and 1945. Later he served as Chief Flying Officer at CFS in the Rhodesian Air Training Group in 1943–5. There were subsequent tours of duty in Münster, Germany (1950), and Cyprus (1956). He was Commanding Officer at Sopley, Hampshire, in 1952, and later stationed at Linton-on-Ouse, Yorkshire (1956), and then Boulmer, Northumberland (1957). He retired in 1959 to Bottesford, Leicestershire, after thirty years' service to the Crown and four monarchs.

He kept up a regular correspondence and a telephone dialogue with Hans Ulrich Kettling. Ted Shipman and Hans Kettling (an Me 110 pilot) first met above Yorkshire on 15 August 1940, when Hans was shot down by Ted. They were subsequently reunited in 1985.

In his retirement the service nickname 'Shippy' was hardly ever used, and he became Ted Shipman once again. He remarried in 1963. He was kept busy with various activities, including working on a voluntary basis with the Civil Defence Corps, the Red Cross, Bottesford Parish Council and St Mary's Church at Bottesford. Ted Shipman actively supported the Air Training Corps (47F at Grantham), the Battle of Britain Fighter Association, the RAF Benevolent Fund, and many other aviation-linked charities and museums. He tried flying again at Tollerton, but found the experience in a modern two-seater aircraft both plain and boring. In his retirement he seldom wished to discuss his exploits and experiences, except when pressed by an enthusiastic researcher, such as Chris Goss.

APPENDIX 1

Air Ministry Records

RAF career chronology[1]

26/05/1930	Joined RAF, Serial No. 512770, AC2, for 8 years
19/01/1931	Remustered driver, petrol
17/03/1933	Remustered AC2 fitter aero engines
01/07/1933	AC1 fitter aero engines
01/01/1934	LAC fitter aero engines
27/01/1936	Remustered pilot under training, service extended to 12 years
06/10/1936	Sergeant remustered pilot fitter aero engines
16/03/1937	Confirmed sergeant fitter aero engines
01/06/1939	Re-engaged for 24 years, flight sergeant
31/03/1940	Emergency commission pilot officer on probation
25/11/1940	Acting flying officer
01/04/1941	Confirmed flying officer
14/10/1941	Acting flight lieutenant
01/04/1942	Flight lieutenant
31/07/1944	Acting squadron leader
05/04/1948	Transferred to Aircraft Control Branch
07/07/1949	Transferred to Fighter Control
18/12/1950	Acting wing commander
19/11/1952	CO RAF Sopley

| 01/01/1955 | Transferred to Ground Branch |
| 09/12/1959 | Retired – retained rank of wing commander |

NOTE

1. Air Ministry Record (Form 1406) Ref. 43364.

History of No. 41 Squadron

Motto: *Seek and Destroy*

Badge: A double-armed cross – approved by HRH King George VI in February 1937. The badge originated from the squadron's association with Saint Omer, France, during the First World War, the cross being part of the town's arms.

Battle Honours: Western Front 1916–1918,* Somme 1916,* Arras, Cambrai 1917,* Somme 1918,* Lys, Amiens,* Battle of Britain 1940,* Home Defence 1940–1944,* Fortress Europe 1940–1944,* Dieppe*, France and Germany 1944–1945,* Arnhem, Walcheren, Gulf 1991.

* Honours marked with an asterisk are emblazoned on the squadron standard.

Number 41 Squadron[1] was formed on 14 July 1916 at Gosport. Two months later, the unit moved to France equipped with FE8s, which proved unsuitable for their intended role as fighters and so were employed on ground-attack missions. During 1917, the squadron received SE5As for fighter and escort duties, although some ground-attack missions were flown to great effect during the German offensive of 1918. Following the Armistice, the unit remained on the continent until February 1919, when it moved to Tangmere and was disbanded at the end of the year. On 1 April 1923, No. 41 Squadron re-formed at Northolt as a fighter squadron, initially equipped with Snipes. These were replaced a year later by Siskins. During the Abyssinian crisis of 1935–6, the squadron found itself in Aden on air-policing duties with two-seat Demons before returning the UK and re-equipping with Furies. In January 1939, No. 41 received its first Spitfires – an association that was, remarkably, to last for the whole of the Second World War. Activity was light for the squadron until May 1940, when it was used to provide fighter cover for the evacuation of Dunkirk and was part of No. 13 Group during the Battle of Britain. In the following years, No. 41 was employed on a variety of missions, including convoy patrol, 'Rhubarb' interdiction flights and fighter interception. After joining the Second Tactical Air Force in September 1944, the squadron flew fighter sweeps over the Continent, moving to Germany as part of the Occupation forces in July 1945. In 1947, the unit spent ten months as an instrument-flying training unit, before reverting to its fighter role and receiving Hornets. The squadron's first jet aircraft, the Meteor, arrived during 1951, and these remained until 1955, when Hunters took over. In 1958, the arrival of all-weather Javelins saw the unit based in East Anglia until disbandment in December 1963. September 1965 saw the squadron re-formed as a Bloodhound surface-to-air missile unit at West Raynham. Changes to the Bloodhound squadrons saw No. 41 disbanded in September 1970, but on 1 April 1972 the squadron re-formed at Coningsby equipped with Phantoms. Jaguars replaced these aircraft in 1977, and the squadron moved to Coltishall. It was disbanded in April 2006.

Note

1. Information from Steve Brew. Web: http://brew.clients.ch/RAF41Sqdn.htm

The Vickers Supermarine Spitfire

Designer: R.J. Mitchell

Specification:
Type: Single-seat fighter
Description: Low-wing monoplane
Wingspan: 36 feet 10 inches (11.23 m)
Length: 29 feet 11 inches (9.12 m)
Height (max): 11 feet 5 inches (3.48 m)
Wing area: 242 square feet (22.48 m^2)
Weight (empty): 4,332 lb (1,965 kg)
Weight (loaded): 5,750 lb (2,609 kg)
Power plant: Rolls-Royce Merlin II V12 liquid-cooled piston engine BHP: 1,030 hp

Armament:
8 fixed wing-mounted 0.303 Browning machine-guns

Performance:
Maximum speed: 362 mph
Initial climb rate: 2,300 ft per min (700 m per min)
Ceiling: 31,900 ft
Range: 395 miles
First flight: 5 March 1936
Service entry: 4 August 1938

Introduction of the Spitfire into Service[1]

At the time of the 1938 Munich Crisis, No. 19 was the only squadron to possess any Spitfires at all. The second unit to receive Spitfires was No. 66 Squadron, also at Duxford, which acquired K9802 on 31 October 1938. Thus, by the end of 1938, the RAF had two fully equipped Spitfire squadrons with 100% reserves. By the outbreak of war on 3 September 1939, Spitfires equipped nine squadrons – Nos 19, 66 and 611 at Duxford, Nos 54, 65 and 74 at Hornchurch, No. 72 at Church Fenton, Nos 41 and 609 at Catterick and No. 602 at Abbotsinch. Additionally, No. 603 Squadron was in the process of replacing its Gladiators at Turnhouse. A total of 306 Mk Is had been delivered, of which thirty-six had been written off in training accidents.

Deliveries of production Spitfire Is began in June 1938, two years after the first production contract had been placed. In those two years Supermarine laid out its Woolston factory for large-scale production, and organised one of the largest sub-contract schemes ever envisaged in Britain until that time, as it was becoming increasingly obvious that there was no limit to the likely demand for the Spitfire. It was also obvious that one factory alone was not going to be able to meet the demand, even with sub-contracting. Large-scale plans were laid during 1937 for the construction by the Nuffield Group of a large new shadow factory at Castle Bromwich, near Birmingham, for Spitfire production. On 12 April 1938 a contract was placed for 1,000 Spitfires to be built at this new factory, of which the actual construction had not then even begun. In the following year, on 29 April, further contracts were placed with Supermarine for 200 Spitfires, and on 9 August for 450. When Britain went to war on 3 September 1939, a total of 2,160 Spitfires were already on order.

The first 77 Mk Is had a two-bladed, fixed-pitch propeller. Subsequent aircraft received three-bladed, two-position airscrews, with fine pitch for take-off and coarse pitch for cruising, and these were subsequently retro-fitted to the earlier aircraft. Taller pilots found the headroom very restrictive, and this led to the original flat cockpit canopy being replaced by the bulged version that was to become a feature of all future marks. Other improvements included the provision of an armour-plated windscreen and 6 mm armour panels on the rear engine bulkhead and behind the pilot's seat. Heating for the guns was also installed after it was found that they froze at high altitude. The original armament of eight .303 Browning machine-guns had been chosen because of the ready availability of this weapon, but in June 1939 two 20 mm Hispano cannon were fitted to L1007 for trials. These proved unsuccessful, as the Hispano had been designed to be mounted on top of a fighter's engine block, which would be solid enough to absorb the recoil. The mountings in the Spitfire's wings were too flexible, causing the guns to jam. Nevertheless, the Hispano was ordered into production, pending a satisfactory solution to this mounting problem.

Many pilots found the new aircraft difficult to adapt to – those used to open cockpits often found the closed canopy claustrophobic and left it fully open. Additionally, these pilots were unfamiliar with the retractable undercarriage, and numerous early accidents were caused by their forgetting to lower the Spitfire's wheels. The aircraft did have a warning klaxon, but as this tended to sound whenever vibration increased, it was often switched off – with embarrassing consequences! Taxiing was a zigzag process requiring the aircraft's tail to be swung from side to side so that the pilot could see ahead beyond the airplane's long nose. Combined with the narrow-track and somewhat fragile undercarriage, this made crosswind landings hazardous. Nevertheless, it was considered that the aircraft could be flown without risk by the average fully trained fighter pilot. New pilots came to the Spitfire via Magister and Master trainers and a short spell at an operational training unit (OTU). Experienced pilots converted to type directly on the squadrons.

Before the outbreak of war, considerable interest in buying Spitfires or arranging licence production had been shown by many foreign countries, including Japan. In the event, one example was flown to the French before war dictated that all future production would be earmarked for the RAF. Orders placed before September 1939 amounted to 1,160 to be built by Supermarine, with a further 1,000 to be produced by the Nuffield organisation.

THE SPITFIRE IN ACTION[2]

On 16 October 1939, Junkers Ju 88s of 1/KG 30 led by *Hauptmann* Helmuth Pohle attacked British warships in the Firth of Forth.

Nine of the Ju 88s were intercepted over Rosyth by three Spitfires of 603 Squadron, each of which attacked Pohle's aircraft, which was hit repeatedly and crashed into the sea.

Pohle was the only survivor and was taken prisoner of war. This, the first enemy aircraft to be destroyed by Fighter Command, was credited to Sqn Ldr Ernest Stevens, the Commanding Officer of 603 Squadron. At the same time, two other sections of 603 Squadron engaged and shot down a Heinkel He 111 which had been sent to observe the results of Pohle's raid. Three more Spitfires, this time from 602 Squadron, were joined by two of 603 in time to catch one more of the Ju 88s and shoot it down. Later that day, another He 111 was shot down by 603 Squadron. Thus did the Spitfire spectacularly open its account against the enemy.

The first enemy aircraft to fall on British soil in the Second World War was a Heinkel He 111, which was shot down at Haddington, East Lothian, on 29 November.

The aircraft was originally attacked by Flg Off Archie McKellar of 602 Squadron, who was then interrupted by the arrival of three Spitfires from 603 Squadron. Although argument rages to this day as to which squadron was the victor, the 'kill' was credited to McKellar.

Spitfires based in England registered their first success when 41 Squadron from Catterick brought down a Heinkel He 111 off Whitby. No. 74 Squadron from Hornchurch scored its first success when three Spitfires attacked a Heinkel He 111 off Southend, and although the Heinkel was not seen to crash, two of its unhappy crew were picked from the sea the next day.

Until this time, photographic reconnaissance was traditionally assigned to bomber-type aircraft. However, the concept of using a small, unarmed aircraft, relying solely on its speed to provide protection, was proposed by Flg Off 'Shorty' Longbotham. The Spitfire was the obvious choice for the task, and the first two Mk Is were converted in October 1939. A five-inch focal length camera was mounted in the in-board gun bay of each wing, inclined so that the field of photography overlapped slightly to give a stereoscopic effect. Stripped of guns, ammunition and radio, and with a high-gloss paint finish, the resulting PR IA was some 30 mph (50 km/h) faster than the standard Spitfire. Contrary to popular belief, the Spitfire was based in France before the Germans overran that country, the Special Survey Flight being established at

Seclin with one PR IA. It flew its first sortie on 18 November, and although the mission was unsuccessful because of adverse weather, it nevertheless proved that the Spitfire was eminently suitable for the task.

Notes

1. Information kindly supplied by Christopher Whitehead – *The Supermarine Spitfire, an Operational History.*
2. Information kindly supplied by Christopher Whitehead – *The Supermarine Spitfire, an Operational History.*

Aircraft Flown by Ted 'Shippy' Shipman

Airspeed Oxford
Avro 504N
Avro Anson
Avro Avian
Avro Lancaster
Avro Tutor
AW Atlas
Beaufighter
Bermuda
Blackburn B2
Blenheim
Buckmaster
Cherokee 140
Cornell
de Havilland Chipmunk
de Havilland Dominie (DH86A)
de Havilland Mosquito
de Havilland Moth 60
de Havilland Moth Minor
de Havilland Tiger Moth
de Havilland Moth 60b
Gloster Gauntlet
Gloster Meteor

Hawker Audax
Hawker Fury II
Hawker Hart T
Hawker Hurricane
Hawker Tomtit
Hotspur
Lockheed Hudson
M18
Master I
Master III
Miles Magister
Mitchell
North American Harvard
Percival Prentice
Redwing
Reliant
Spartan
Vickers Supermarine Spitfire Mk I, Mk II and Mk V
Vickers Valentia
Wellington 1C
Whitley

Summary of Flying by Ted 'Shippy' Shipman

Flying all types:

Flying time on forty-nine different types of aircraft, of which forty-six were as pilot:

Single-engined aircraft:	2,565 hours, 40 minutes
Multi-engined aircraft:	1,041 hours, 00 minutes
Total:	3,606 hours, 40 minutes

Of which

Day-flying hours were:	3,339 hours, 15 minutes
Night-flying hours were:	267 hours, 25 minutes
Number of separate flights recorded:	4,409
Number of take-offs and landings:	9,000–10,000 (estimated)

Spitfire flying:

First flight:
12 January 1939, 1 hour, 10 minutes; Spitfire Mk I K9835, fixed-pitch, two-bladed, wooden propeller

Total Spitfire flying time:
On types Mk I, Mk II and Mk V: 317 hours, 14 minutes

Translation of a Letter from Bernhard Hochstuhl to Ted Shipman, 11 July 1990

Dear Ted,

Many thanks for your letter dated 9/3/90. Please allow me to write to you in German as I am out of practice in English. I am very much in contact with Eugen Lange but we are not in such good shape regarding health, and this makes writing difficult. In May I went to the POW reunion which takes place in the Black Forest. I now wish to tell you briefly my whereabouts in England and Canada. In Whitby Eugen and I stayed in the hospital for two or three days. I do remember very clearly that two RAF officers visited us and gave us some cigarettes. These two gentlemen were adamant that they were the ones who shot us down, and we had to believe them. We exchanged addresses, which were lost in the years afterwards.

Later I was in London for interrogation for fourteen days and also in the West End. In the Royal Herbert Hospital in London I underwent a leg operation but my shrapnel is still in my leg.

Just before Christmas 1939 I was transferred to the POW camp in Oldham. The majority of prisoners were from U-boats. In May 1940 the prisoners were transferred to Canada. Rumours circulated that the English Crown Jewels were being transported at the same time.

Next I was an interpreter with a work party in Quebec which was to build an internment camp. Approximately eight weeks later I was transferred to the main camp, Espanola, by Gudburg. There I met up with Eugen again. I stayed about two years behind barbed wire. To pass the time we received lessons in languages, mathematics and science.

In approximately 1943 I was transferred to Alberta, along with 1,200 prisoners. I volunteered as a lumberjack to get to know the beautiful country.

In 1945 I got to South Ontario to work on the land. At Christmas 1946 I was sent to Oldham UK for a few weeks. Then I went and worked on the aerodrome in Bicester, near Oxford. On one Saturday afternoon I refused to work and sent the workers home. I had to see the Commanding Officer, who asked where and by whom we were shot down. The Sergeant Major said that those pilots were no longer alive.

In autumn 1947 I came back to my parents. After a few years' apprenticeship and study I was employed as an engineer for twenty-eight years with the firm Siemens in Karlsruhe, which is now a twin city to Nottingham.

In 1975 I lost one eye through a tumour, and at the moment I have only 8% vision in the other eye. Hence I can't go out on my own. My wife must always be at my side.

But you are few years older than I am and must also have some problems with your health. So for now I send my good wishes to you and your wife, and especially wish you good health.

Yours truly,
Bernhard

Appendix 7

Transcript from Durham Police Occurrence Book for 15 August 1940

<u>Thursday 15th August 1940</u>

<u>Two German Airmen brought to Police Office under escort</u>

At 14.10 hrs today, two German Airmen, an officer and an NCO, were brought to this office under Police and Military Guard, having been taken prisoner from their aeroplane which was shot down by a British Spitfire near Streatham Gap, Strindrop, about 13.30 hrs today.

The officer had slight burns to his right hand. The NCO had a slight bullet wound in right knee. Both men received attention from the Military Medical Officer. The prisoners were kept separate and no persons were allowed to question them. They were later interrogated by an RAF officer (Intelligence).

German officer left this office at 23.00 hrs under escort. German NCO left this office at 16.30 hrs on Saturday 17th August 1940, under military escort.

Signed. Sgt 142 Campbell

APPENDIX 8

Transcript from Dennis Knight's[1] Notes Relating to 15 August 1940

13.20 hours approx.   15th August 1940
                                                        Co. Durham

<u>Messerschmitt 110 crashed at Streatham Nr Barnard Castle</u>

M8 + CH 1/ZG 76 Disc No. 53591 O/Lt Ketling + one (O/Gefr Volk)

This machine was brought down as the result of machine-gun fire from a British fighter. Over the Durham and North Riding of Yorkshire borders the aircraft glided down to belly-land 2½ Mile N.E. of Barnard Castle near Streatham Castle entrance.

This aircraft was a long-range fighter specially adapted for the long flight over the North Sea from Norway escorting Heinkels attacking Tyne-Tees targets. This particular machine having penetrated inland to Barnard Castle would not have been able to complete the return journey back over the North Sea.

[Interviews Bernard Castle 2/8/67]

Fred Nevison who is proprietor of a gentleman's outfitters in Bernard Castle lived at 'Byeways', Abbey Lane, Startforth, saw the German fighter break cloud N.E. of Barnard Castle and go down over the town to crash near the Bishop Auckland road, opposite the gates to Streatham Castle.

William Nelson a local plumber recalled the incident. He was at the time working at the army camps of Streatham and Stainton which were being built on the 15th August 1940. He heard aircraft and machine-gun fire above the clouds and saw a twin-engined aircraft appear out of the clouds and fly towards the camp where he was working. It lost height and circled the camp, its black crosses being plainly visible. No British aircraft could be seen although Mr Nevison said he saw one behind the Messerschmitt when it flew over Startforth [Bennions?].

Nelson watched as the German aircraft rocked its wings and started to come in to land. When near the ground the plane put its nose down and dived, just flattening out to belly-land behind the camp sewage works. The aircraft careered through a hedge and came to rest in a cloud of dust. Some 50 to 60 workmen were on the camp site and they ran towards the aircraft, Nelson being one of those in the van. However, they hesitated when they saw tall Germans standing outside their aircraft firing automatic pistols at it in attempt to set it alight. Seeing the workmen however the Germans lifted their hands above their heads and the horde ran forward to converge on the airmen. In the excitement that followed an argument arose – one workman being bent on cutting the Germans' throats.

Mr Nelson noticed that the Germans were not wearing flying helmets and had peaked caps. The aircraft was painted a darkish mouse colour with crosses and it had been hit by at least 40 bullets. One of the Germans was very tall and appeared to be senior to the other.

Nelson climbed onto the cockpit leaning into the cockpit, he tugged a handle and pulled out the inflatable rubber dinghy pack and made off with it to his workshop, for which he was later brought up before the local magistrate and fined £2 0s 0d. He said that the dinghy wouldn't have worked because it had bullets through it.

Police and troops arrived and cordoned off the area, the airmen being taken to Barnard Castle police station. Mr Nelson said that later during the day an RAF pilot who was supposed to have shot the Germans down came over from Catterick aerodrome and saw the prisoners.

The aircraft caught fire some 30 minutes after it crashed and exploding ammunition wounded one or two people.

NOTE

1. Dennis Knight, Round Lodge, Buckland Court, Betchworth, Surrey, 1967.

Extracts from a Letter from Hans Kettling to Ted Shipman, January 1980

Blumenstrasse 4
402 Mettman
Germany
6.01.80

Dear Mr Shipman

From our mutual young letter friend and researcher Christopher Goss I learned that you (and/or Mr Bennions) were the pilots who on 15.8.1940 brought down a German Me Bf 110 M8-CH near Barnard Castle, of which I was the pilot. He gave me your address and got me to understand that you might be interested to hear from me. Well, here I am, safe and sound, and forty years after we became acquainted for a few seconds in mid-air.

I think it is a little bit late now to give you my congratulations. Instead of this, and since our short rendezvous was apt to change the course of my life entirely, you might be more interested to hear how everything went on.

After two weeks of interrogation at Cockfosters[1] (and a nice healing of the burns on my hand) I was sent with several other officer POWs to Grizedale Hall, where I met a bunch of air and navy men, also parachuters, who were the lucky ones to survive, some of them being able to tell hair-raising stories. Thanks to you and your friends a steady supply of POWs came in daily at that time, and we next celebrated Christmas, always waiting for the church bells to ring, which would indicate a German invasion. At the end of January 1941 we were shipped to Canada aboard the 'Duchess of York', where I was glad to meet Mr Volk, my wireless operator and gunner, well restored, only a slight limp showing the effects of the wounding. We left ship at Halifax in midwinter, and I remember the newspaper boys shouting, 'Tobruk fallen.' Going by railway for several days and nights, some of the POWs managed to jump for freedom out of the windows, but lots of snow and extreme cold made them forget their intentions. All came back, sooner or later, except Oblt. Franz U. Werra, who was lucky and kept going enough to cross the St Lawrence over the ice and by boat, and who eventually reached the still neutral USA, and later Germany.

The following years I spent in different camps, from Lake Ontario to the Rocky Mountains. After some initial differences between guardians and POWs on the question of whether to treat us as criminals or as defeated soldiers, we went along very fine with the Canadian Veteran Guard, and after a while they even let us walk and roam in uninhabited parts of the country on parole, which they found 'as good as a Canadian dollar'.

It was in these years of leisure, realising that there would be no more flying for me after the war, that I found pleasure in creating handsome things from all sorts of materials. The Red Cross did a lot of help and encouragement with tools and materials.

After repatriation in November 1946, including some months of awful experiences in post-war England, I found my way back to my family. I had made up mind to earn my bread and butter (there was none!) as a craftsman, and I was lucky again in finding a well-known master bookbinder, who was willing to take on a thirty-year-old ex-pilot as an apprentice. . . .

So I would be very interested to hear from you, how you went along during the war and afterwards, but only if you find the time and a liking for it. . . .

Yours very truly
Hans Ulrich Kettling

Note

1. Trent Park, Cockfosters, Barnet, London EN4, which was from December 1939 to July 1942 the Combined Services Detailed Interrogation Centre (CSDIC). Captured *Luftwaffe* aircrews were thought to be more susceptible to talk straight after landing, while still in a state of shock. Interrogation officers were located at RAF stations throughout the country to proceed to the site of any crash. They would interview survivors and decide whether certain prisoners would be sent to Trent Park for further interrogation.

Eyewitness Accounts from the Ground, 15 August 1940

The following are eyewitness accounts from various people on the ground, listening to and watching the battle in the skies above Barnard Castle on 15 August 1940.[1]

Alan Byde:[2]

I was a boy of twelve in a field near to Stainton. It was harvest time for crops and souls. The light luminous cloud layer was 10/10 complete and high. The stutter of guns was clearly heard and two or three aircraft could be seen swooping out of the cloud base and tearing back into the air fleet above the cloud.

Some children came along and said there was a German aircraft down in the fields at the back of Barford Camp. We cycled there via the railway track from Broomielaw Station. The Me 110 was south of the railway. The aircraft was burning. There was the intermittent stutter of gunfire as the heat of the fire exploded ammunition. We lay in a ditch until the firing had stopped. When we arrived at the wreckage, children, a policeman and workmen from the camp were gathered around. Children were gathering up live rounds of ammunition including cannon shells. A young Army officer stood on the wingtip and called us all around him and told us what could happen. We carefully laid a large heap of shells at his feet.

A man was standing near the leading edge of the starboard wing and with a 'wumph' some shells came out and struck him on the chest. He was knocked over and while conscious he bled. Soldiers bound his wound.

I was told that after the aircraft crash-landed some local workmen climbed into the aircraft and took out the radio, the inflatable dinghy and other odds and ends. The German crew watched them. The workmen took away their souvenirs. The airmen then set the plane on fire.

We hung around for an hour or two. One boy showed me two burned oxygen cylinders and later other boys showed me machine-gun belt-feed clips and cartridges. Some boys fired these cartridges using a nail and hammer and were lucky not to be injured. I had some cartridges and my uncle prised them apart with pliers. As soon as the contents met the air they blazed into flame, as they were incendiaries or tracers.

Mr Wright:[3]

On the 15th August 1940 the Me 110 aircraft crash-landed close by where Barford Camp was being built. It struck a pole that carried an overhead power line to Barnard Castle. The resultant interruption to the electrical supply required the 'all clear' to be sounded in Barnard Castle by the ringing of hand-bells. After the crash one aircraft crew member held some Barford building workers at bay with a gun while the other fired the aircraft to destroy it. A postman friend saw the dogfight.

Mr Kendal Mason, Osmond Croft Farm, Winston:[4]

I was 11 years old and I was in a farmyard on the 15th August 1940. It was a fine sunny day where father was a helper working with the sheep at Oak Lea Farm. We heard aircraft about and then the sound of machine-guns as two were seen chasing another. We could see it all without any bother as they wheeled and fired. One fighter, still firing, followed the plane down after smoke started coming from an engine. We were excited by it all and we were severely reprimanded for being in the open due to the dangers of stray bullets and shrapnel.

As soon as we saw the plane go down the man who was helping father and I were off to see where it was down. It had landed about a mile way to the north-west. By the time we got there it was on fire and shells were exploding from it. Soldiers would not let us near it. Within a fortnight the crash site had been cleared.

Fred Lee, Middle Farm, Holwick, Middleton:[5]

I was six years of age and on the 15th August 1940 I was at Holwick Village School. I recall my father telling me that a German plane and pursuer came from the north-east – the Spitfire pumping shells into the raider. Bullets struck the door of the house opposite the school. Father was sufficiently worried that he rushed to the school to check if all was OK.

My uncle was working at Streatham and when the plane came down a number of workers rushed forward. They were held at bay by the pilot with a pistol until the crew had fired the plane.

Elsie Bayles, 44 The Oval, Barnard Castle:[6]

In August 1940 I was living as a 21-year-old servant girl at Gill Fields Farm near Romaldkirk. I was in the farmyard, talking to the grocer from Middleton, who was making a delivery. I was unaware of anything amiss until I heard the clatter of metallic objects falling into the yard from the sky. These might have been shell cases. As I stood looking skyward I heard the sound of aircraft overhead and then I saw two aircraft quite low, one chasing another and moving in the general direction of Barnard Castle.

The air battle overhead and the spent shell cases falling to the ground frightened the farm horses.

George Richardson, Fair View Farm, Long Newton:[7]

I was a 14-year-old schoolboy in August 1940. I was living with a family at East Whorley Hill Farm, two miles west of

Winston on the Barnard Castle road. Harvest was on and I had just arrived in a field to help my father at about 1.00 p.m., when I heard the sound of gunfire in the sky. I could not see anything as it was cloudy, though the weather was fine. I had to return to the farmhouse on an errand. As I did so I heard a dull drone of many aircraft flying high above the cloud. I heard further gunfire. I took cover behind a tree as shell cases started falling around me. I saw a plane glide out from the clouds, apparently following the course of the Tees river – westwards towards Barnard Castle. I recall seeing fighters in attendance. I lost sight of the plane – a German Me 110, as it got lower and then disappeared behind the landscape.

Douglas Bradbrook:[8]

I was six years old in August 1940 and attending Wycliffe RC School, Hutton Magna, near Whorlton. I heard the sound of heavy machine-gun fire about a mile away, and ignoring the teacher's cries for all to seek cover under the school desks we ran outside to see.

I saw a plane, which was an Me 110, at about 2,000 feet trailing smoke as it passed over the school in the direction of Wycliffe and Barnard Castle. It was low enough to see the crew. Two fighters followed. I learned that the plane had crash-landed near Barford Camp which was under construction and close to Broomielaw railway station. My grandfather, William Walker, was a building worker on the site. He cycled over to our house and showed me a bar of German chocolate.

NOTES

1. Supplied by Bill Norman.
2. Recorded in 1988.
3. Recorded in 1989.
4. Recorded in 1989.
5. Recorded in 1989.
6. Recorded in 1990.
7. Recorded in 1990.
8. Recorded in 1990.

Appendix 11

Luftwaffe Organisation

The *Luftwaffe*[1] equivalent of the squadron was the *Staffel*, also consisting of approximately twelve aircraft, in this instance Messerschmitt Bf 109s. Unlike its Royal Air Force equivalents, a *Gruppe* of three *Staffeln* formed the basic operational unit, with each *Staffel* linked administratively and operationally. This is unlike the Royal Air Force wing, which consisted of aircraft from whichever adjacent squadrons were available at any particular time. Generally, three or more *Gruppen* then formed a *Geschwader*.

Each *Geschwader* was prefixed with a title relating to its operational role. Fighter units were designated *Jagdgeschwader* (abbreviated JG). *Staffeln* within a *Jagdgeschwader* were sub-divided into groups of four aircraft, known as a *Schwarm*. Within each *Schwarm*, as with RAF sections, the aircraft were split into two *Rotten* (pairs). The leader of each *Rotte* was known as the *Rottenführer*, and his wingman the *Rottenflieger*. The chief responsibility of the *Rottenflieger* was to defend his leader from attack. The leader would also provide cover for his *Rottenflieger* but would also be responsible for navigation.

Within the *Schwarm*, the leading *Rottenführer* would also be the *Schwarmführer*. The *Schwarm* was also referred to as the 'Finger Four', and allowed much greater offensive strength and formation flexibility, particularly when manoeuvring as a *Staffel*. This was in contrast to the Royal Air Force formations of four groups of three aircraft, which required more rigid adherence to the formation arrangement to avoid collision or breaking of the formation.

In addition, the *Staffel* was not maintained on a horizontal plane, such as with RAF formations, but stepped up at different levels for tactical advantage. With the twelve aircraft virtually line abreast, the fighters were less conspicuous to ground or air observation and offered each other better protection.

Each individual aircraft maintained its service identity, irrespective of its operational assignment, by carrying a manu-facturer's plate with a four-figure manufacturer's serial number – the *Werk Nummer*. In most cases, this serial was also stencilled on the rudder assembly. The aircraft's identity within the *Staffel* bore a single number painted in the *Staffel* colour on the forward side of the cross on each side of the fuselage.

Staffeln within a *Geschwader* were uniquely numbered: 1, 2, 3 *Staffeln* formed I *Gruppe*; 4, 5, 6 *Staffeln* formed II *Gruppe*; and 7, 8, 9 *Staffeln* formed III *Gruppe*. Thus 3/JG52 was the third *Staffel*, belonging to I *Gruppe*, in *Jagdgeschwader* 52.

A colour code was incorporated into the unit markings in order to identify individual *Staffeln* within each *Gruppe*: white numbers represented the first *Staffel* in each *Gruppe* (1, 4, 7 *Staffeln*); red represented the second *Staffel* in each *Gruppe* (2, 5, 8 *Staffeln*); yellow represented the third *Staffel* within the *Gruppe* (3, 6, 9 *Staffeln*).

The *Gruppe* was identified by a symbol on the opposite side of the cross. A horizontal or vertical bar represented II *Gruppe*; a wavy line represented III *Gruppe*; and a blank space represented I *Gruppe*. *Gruppe* and *Geschwader* flights for aircraft other than fighters used green and blue identification codes.

A *Gruppe Kommandeur*'s staff *Stab* was the *Gruppe*'s head-quarters unit, and included an HQ flight *Stabsschwarm* of four aircraft which he led on operations. Staff aircraft and unit leaders used a combination of chevron and bar symbols in place of the individual aircraft number. For example, < to represent the *Gruppe* Adjutant, and <– to represent the *Gruppe Kommandeur*'s aircraft. The particular *Geschwader* to which an aircraft belonged could only be determined by a small motif painted on the fuselage sides to the front of the cockpit, which might be representative of a particular *Geschwader* or was unique to one of the *Staffeln* or *Gruppen* within it.

The designation of individual aircraft, *Staffel* and *Geschwader* for other *Luftwaffe* units was similar to that adopted for fighters.

Bombers were titled *Kampfgeschwader* (*KG*); dive-bombers *Stuka-geschwader* (*StG*); 'destroyer' units (twin-engined fighters, such as the Bf 110) *Zerstorergeschwader* (*ZG*); and operational training units *Lehrgeschwader* (*LG*). The *Geschwader* might consist of *Gruppen* of varying aircraft types and tactical roles.

Staffeln within a *Kampfgeschwader* were formed into separate *Ketten* consisting of three aircraft aligned in arrowhead formation. As with fighter formations, each *Gruppe* had a staff flight – *Stabskette*. *Staffeln* consisting of Me 110 aircraft were sub-divided into *Schwarm* formation, as with single-seat fighters.

Markings on bombers and *Zerstorer* aircraft consisted of four characters, with two each side of the national cross. The two characters to the left of the cross consisted of a number and letter combination which designated the *Kampfgeschwader* to which the aircraft was assigned. For example, U5 would specify *KG2*. The two figures to the right of the cross identified the individual aircraft and the *Staffel* to which it was assigned.

As with fighter markings, the *Staffel* was specified by painting or outlining the individual letter allocated to that particular aircraft in the *Staffel* colour.

Note

1. Kindly provided by Philip Harvey.

Notes on Each Pilot Mentioned

Kindly provided by Steve Brew

Name	**BENNIONS, George Herman** 'Ben'
Number	563057/43354
Rank	Sergeant Pilot/Pilot Officer
Nationality	British
Arrived	16 February 1936
Departed	1 October 1940
Decorations	DFC (1940)
Notes	Born Burslem, Staffs., 13 March 1913; cannon shell exploded in cockpit, blinding him in one eye and wounding his right arm and leg; baled-out and hospitalised; underwent plastic surgery at Queen Victoria Hospital, East Grinstead, by pioneering Dr Archie McIndoe; became one of the famous 'Guinea Pigs'; died 30 January 2004; see also 'On Being Shot Down', Combat Report for 17 September 1940, and 'George Bennions: 15 March 1913 to 30 January 2004, An Obituary'.

Name	**BLATCHFORD, Howard Peter** 'Cowboy''
Number	37715
Rank	Pilot Officer, Flying Officer
Nationality	Canadian
Arrived	10 January 1937
Departed	20 April 1940
Decorations	DFC (1940)

Notes Shared with Sgts E.A. Shipman and A. Harris 41 Squadron's first WWII victory, an He 111 destroyed over the North Sea, approx. twenty miles from shore, 17 October 1939; KIA,[1] 3 May 1943, aged 31; son of Kenneth A. and Grace L. Blatchford, of Edmonton, Alta, Canada; remembered on Panel 118 of the Runnymede Memorial.

Name **CARR-LEWTY, Robert Albert**
Number 580095
Rank Sergeant Pilot
Nationality British
Arrived October 1937
Departed Unknown
Decorations AFC (1945)
Notes Relinquished commission, July 1956, retaining Flight Lieutenant.

Name **CARTER, Leslie Raymond**
Number 754236
Rank Sergeant Pilot
Nationality British
Arrived 1 October 1940
Departed Early 1941
Notes KIA with 74 Squadron, 6 July 1941, aged 21; son of Albert W. and Jeanetta C. Carter, of Shenley, Herts.; remembered on Panel 35 of the Runnymede Memorial.

Name **COPLEY, James John Hawke**
Number 41258
Rank Pilot Officer
Nationality British
Arrived 10 June 1939
Departed 14 September 1939
Notes KIFA,[2] 14 September 1939, aged 18; son of Sqn Ldr Reginald J. and Josephine M. Copley of Newton, Cambridgeshire; buried in Newton St Margaret Churchyard, Newton, Cambridgeshire.

Name	**CORY, Guy Webster**
Number	40677
Rank	Pilot Officer
Nationality	British
Arrived	17 December 1938
Departed	*c.* late 1940
Decorations	AFC (1942)
Notes	Born 2 September 1916; retired July 1954, retaining Wing Commander.

Name	**DARLING, Edward Vivian** 'Mitzi'
Number	Unknown/65979
Rank	Sergeant Pilot/Pilot Officer
Nationality	British
Arrived	17 December 1939
Departed	12 June 1941
Decorations	DFC (1941)
Notes	Commissioned January 1941; KIA, 2 June 1942; remembered on Panel 65 of the Runnymede Memorial.

Name	**DARRANT, John Stewart**
Number	242508
Rank	Warrant Officer
Nationality	British
Arrived	Prior to 8 December 1939, when recommended for a commission
Departed	*c.* May 1940
Decorations	MiD (1941), MiD (1942), MiD (1944), OBE (1946)
Notes	Born 4 November 1899; commissioned in Technical Branch, May 1940; retired September 1953, retaining Wing Commander.

Name	**FORD, Roy Clement** 'Henry'
Number	741683/88214
Rank	Sergeant Pilot/Pilot Officer
Nationality	British
Arrived	16 December 1939
Departed	15 April 1941

Decorations Unknown
Notes   Commissioned late November 1940; released from
                RAF, October 1945 and commissioned in RAFVR,
                September 1947; retired May 1952; died December
                2002.

Name   **GAMBLEN, Douglas Robert**
Number   39657
Rank   Acting Pilot Officer, Pilot Officer, Flying Officer
Nationality British
Term 1   27 November 1937 to 10 June 1938
Term 2   7 February 1939 to 29 July 1940
Notes   KIA over Dover, 29 July 1940; remembered on
                Panel 5 of the Runnymede Memorial.

Name   **HARRIS, Albert** 'Bill'
Number   563150
Rank   Sergeant Pilot
Nationality British
Arrived   5 July 1936
Departed   18 October 1939
Notes   Born Cambridge, England, 18 October 1912; shared
                with Flg Off H.P. Blatchford and Sgt E.A. Shipman
                41 Squadron's first WWII victory, an He 111
                destroyed over North Sea, approx. twenty miles
                from shore, 17 October 1939; KIFA, 18 October 1939,
                aged 27; son of Arthur and Eva Harris, husband of
                Violet A. Harris, of Toronto, Ont., Canada; buried
                in South Hinksey (St Laurence) Churchyard, Berks.,
                Section O, Grave 209; see also '41 Squadron
                Casualties in a 102 Squadron Bomber'.

Name   **HOOD, Hilary Richard Lionel** 'Robin'
Number   26110
Rank   Squadron Leader
Nationality British
Arrived   20 April 1940
Departed   5 September 1940
Decorations DFC (1940)

Notes	CO, 20 April to 5 September 1940; born Paddington, London, 13 May 1908; KIFA, 5 September 1940, aged 32; son of John L.B. and Helene M. Hood, née Lessels; remembered on Panel 4 of the Runnymede Memorial. See also 'His True Fate Revealed?'; 'Accounts of his Loss by Various Observers'; 'His Life and Career, Through the Eyes of His Colleagues'; and Significant Flying Log Book Entries.

Name	**HOWITT, Isaac Edward**
Number	580341
Rank	Sergeant Pilot
Nationality	British
Arrived	August 1937
Departed	15 December 1940
Decorations	Unknown
Notes	–

Name	**LANGLEY, Gerald Archibald**
Number	81641
Rank	Pilot Officer
Nationality	British
Arrived	18 June 1940
Departed	15 September 1940
Notes	SD and KIA, 15 September 1940, aged 24; son of Archibald F.M. and Mary E. Langley of Northampton; buried in Grave 1300 of Abington (SS Peter and Paul) Churchyard, Northants.

Name	**LEGARD, William Ernest 'Billy'**
Number	34045
Rank	Flying Officer
Nationality	British
Arrived	26 November 1939
Departed	1 June 1940
Notes	SD and KIA, 1 June 1940, aged 29; son of Digby and Elaine Legard, & husband of Alice Legard of York; remembered on Panel 6 of the Runnymede Memorial.

Name	**LOCK, Eric Stanley** 'Sawn Off'/'Lockie'
Number	81642
Rank	Pilot Officer
Nationality	British
Arrived	18 June 1940
Departed	17 November 1940
Decorations	DFC (1940), Bar to DFC (1940), DSO (1940)
Notes	Born Bayston Hill, near Shrewsbury, 1920; KIA near Calais with 611 Squadron, 3 August 1941; remembered on Panel 29 of the Runnymede Memorial.

Name	**LOVELL, Anthony Desmond Joseph**
Number	40402
Rank	Flying Officer, Flight Lieutenant
Nationality	British
Term 1	20 August 1938 (attached to SHQ Catterick for Admin. Duties, 22 July to 20 November 1939, attached to 53 OTU Heston, 20–24 February 1941)
Term 2	October 1941
Decorations	DFC (1940), Bar to DFC (1942), DSO (1942), US DFC (1944), Bar to DSO (1945)
Notes	Born 9 August 1919; KIFA at Old Sarum, 17 August 1945, aged 26; son of Stuart C.A. and Clare M. Lovell, of Portrush, Northern Ireland; buried in Portrush Cemetery, Co. Antrim, Section F, Grave 1153; see also 'The Crash of Flying Officer Anthony D.J. Lovell, 1940'.

Name	**MACKENZIE, John Noble**
Number	40547
Rank	Pilot Officer
Nationality	New Zealander
Term 1	17 September 1938 to 9 March 1941 (485 Squadron, Driffield, 9–25 March 1941)
Term 2	25 March to September 1941
Decorations	DFC (1941)
Notes	Born Goodwood, Otago, NZ, 11 August 1914; commissioned in RAF as Flight Lieutenant, July 1946; retired December 1957, retaining Squadron Leader.

Name	**MORROGH-RYAN, Oliver Bertram**
Number	40970
Rank	Flying Officer
Nationality	British
Arrived	15 April 1939
Departed	1940
Notes	KIA (68 Squadron), 26 July 1941, aged 22; son of Leonard and Laura Morrogh-Ryan, and husband of Marguerite Morrogh-Ryan of Brettanby Manor; buried in Grave 26 of the Lower Plot of Barton (St Cuthbert) Churchyard, Yorks.

Name	**OVERALL, Horace Ernest Herbert** 'Pooky'
Number	39331
Rank	Flying Officer
Nationality	Canadian
Arrived	7 August 1937
Departed	6 November 1939
Notes	KIFA, 6 November 1939, aged 26; son of William J. and Annie S. Overall of Niagara Falls, Ont., Canada; buried in Catterick Cemetery, Yorks., Church of England Section, Row M, Grave 4.

Name	**RYDER, Edgar Norman**
Number	39193
Rank	Pilot Officer, Flying Officer, Flight Lieutenant
Nationality	British
Arrived	30 June 1937 (attached SHQ Catterick for Admin. Duties, 7 February to 22 July 1939)
Departed	Early 1941?
Decorations	DFC (1940), Bar to DFC (1941), MiD (1945)
Notes	Born 28 November 1914; SD and captured (Kenley Wing), 31 October 1941; held in *Stalag Luft* III (POW No. 658), 1944; retired October 1960, retaining Group Captain.

Name	**SAYERS, James Edgar** 'Jimmy'
Number	Unknown
Rank	Sergeant Pilot, Flight Sergeant
Nationality	British

Arrived	September 1935
Departed	October 1940
Decorations	Unknown
Notes	Remustered to engine fitter, October 1940; discharged from RAF, January 1953, as Warrant Officer.

Name	**SHIPMAN, Edward Andrew** 'Shippy'
Number	512770/43364
Rank	Sergeant Pilot, Flight Sergeant/Pilot Officer
Nationality	British
Arrived	10 October 1936
Departed	19 October 1940
Decorations	AFC (1945)
Notes	Born 9 December 1909; commissioned April 1940; retired December 1959, retaining Wing Commander; died August 1998.

Name	**STAPLETON, William**
Number	41078
Rank	Pilot Officer
Nationality	British
Arrived	30 November 1939
Departed	1 June 1940
Decorations	OBE (1965)
Notes	Born 27 June 1920; SD and captured, 1 June 1940; held in *Stalag Luft* III (POW No. 50), 1944; retired September 1964, retaining Wing Commander.

Name	**USMAR, Frank**
Number	741735
Rank	Sergeant Pilot
Nationality	British
Arrived	18 June 1940
Departed	27 September 1940
Decorations	MiD (1945)
Notes	Born 16 September 1915; commissioned December 1941; retired September 1964, retaining Squadron Leader.

Name	**WALLENS, Ronald Walter** 'Wally'
Number	70708
Rank	Pilot Officer, Flying officer
Nationality	British
Term 1	26 March to August 1938
Term 2	7 October 1938 to 5 September 1940
Decorations	DFC (1944)
Notes	See also 'The Crash of Pilot Officer R.W. 'Wally' Wallens, 1940'

Name	**WEBSTER, John Terence** 'Terry'
Number	37436
Rank	Pilot Officer, Flying Officer, Flight Lieutenant
Nationality	British
Arrived	11 April 1938
Departed	5 September 1940
Decorations	DFC (1940)
Notes	Born Liverpool, 20 March 1916; KIFA during combat in MAC with Flt Lt R.E. Lovett of 73 Squadron, 5 September 1940; remembered on Panel 4 of the Darlington Memorial in Durham. See also 'The Loss of Flight Lieutenant John T. Webster, 1940'

NOTES

1. KIA: killed in action.
2. KIFA: killed in flying accident.

APPENDIX 13

Names of Persons Mentioned in the Text

Acott
Adams, J.S.L.
Andrews, Sgt
Angus
Appleton
Armfield, Sam
Armfield, Brenda
Atcherley, R.L.R.
Bachle, Alfred
Baker, Dizzy
Barker, Jack
Barkham, Lofty
Barrard, H.R.
Barton, Butch
Beamont, Roland
Behnisch, Rudolf
Bennions, Ben George
Benson
Berry, J.
Bishop
Black
Blake
Blatchford, Cowboy
Booth, Howarth
Boret, J.A.

Boxall
Boyle, John
Bridgeman
Brook-Popham, Robert
Brothers
Burton, Titch
Campbell
Carr-Lewty
Carter
Chamberlain, Neville
Chinnoty
Chiswell, Peter
Christ, Kurt
Churchill, Winston
Clark, John
Clayton, Jack
Cockley, L.H.
Coleman, Dusty
Coltart
Conyers, J.
Copley, James
Cory
Coward, James
Crisham, Paddy
Cudgeman

D'Arcy Greig
Darling, Mitzi Edward
Dawson
Donaldson, Baldy
Dring, Frank
Dunning, John
Durrant
Edge
Embry, Basil
Fewtrell
Finlay, Donald
Ford, Henry Roy
Gamblen, D.R.
Gascoigne
Gaut, Acker
Gebhardt, *Gefreiter*
Gibbs, D.
Gillan, John
Glew
Goss, Chris
Gregory
Groncher
Guisborough, Lord
Hamer
Hamilton, Jock
Hammond
Harris, Bill
Hay, Will
Hefele, Hans
Hemsley
Henkel, Otto
Hochsthul, Bernhard
Holman, Les
Holmes, Tealeaf
Hood, Robin
Howitt, Ted
Hunn
Hurst, G.
Jeff, Dorethea
Jenkinson

Jones, Horace
Keegan
Kempe, Georg
Keraghan
Kettling, Hans Ulrich
Kettling, Margaret
Kiank, Hans
Kime
Kingsford-Smith, Charles
Knott
Knowles
Kretschmer, Joachim
Lacey, Ginger Ted
Lange, Eugen
Langley, G.
Law, Elsie
Lawrence, T.E.
Le Marchant Brock, H.M.
Le Rougetel, Willie
le Voi
Leathart, James
Lee
Legard, Billy
Leigh-Mallory
Lent, Helmut
Lewis, Dudley
Lock, Sawn-off Eric
Longman, Sir Arthur
Loobes, Gustav
Lorimer
Lovell, Lulu
Luckman, Reginald
MacDonald, D.S.M.
MacIndoe, Archibald
MacKenzie, John
McGregor-Watt, P.
McIntyre, R.V.
McKeard
McMillan
Mamer

Manners, Lord
Martyn
Mears
Miller
Mitchell, Kenneth
Molders, Werner
Morgan, Taffy
Morrogh-Ryan
Nelson, R.
Newall, Cyril
O'Keefe, Paddy
Oldfield, Barney
Oldmeadow
Olley
Overall, Pooky
Packer
Park, Keith
Partridge, Birdie
Patch, Sam Hubert
Pearson
Pennington-Leigh
Peterson, Charles
Powell
Ppeiffer, Georg
Pride
Probyn, Daddy
Pryde
Reed-Purvis, Harry
Restemeyer, *Hauptmann*
Riedel, Hermann
Roberts
Robertson
Roman
Roulston
Russell
Ryan, Buck
Ryder
Ryder, Norman
Rye, Joe
Satherly

Sauer, Hugo
Saul, R.E.
Sayers, Jimmy
Scarf, Pongo
Seale
Shales, F.H.
Shillito
Smeddle
Smith, Walter
Speare
Spotswood, Dennis
Stapleton, Bill
Staton, W.E.
Stephan, *Hauptmann*
Stern
Stevens
Stewart
Strong
Sullivan
Sumner
Tapper, Ken
Therlmann
Thomas, George
Usmar, Frank
Ussbaum, Fritz
Vincent, Arthur
Volk, *O/Gefr*
von Besser, Horst
Wallace, G.
Wallens, Wally
Watt, Jimmy
Weber, Albert
Webster, John
Wells, Hawkeye
Wilson, Roland
Wilson, Winifred
Wolf
Wolfien, Gunther
Womphrey, Eddie

Diagrams

Modified RAF 'vic' formation

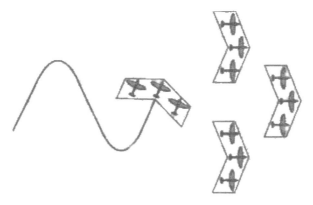

Three widely spaced 'vics' in arrowhead formation,
followed by a fourth weaving 'vic', allowed better
look out capability and manoeuvrability than the tight
'vic' formation.

RAF formation for one 'section' of three aircraft

A single aircraft would maintain a weaving pattern behind the leader
and the wingman. The trailing aircraft had three disadvantages: (1) fuel
consumption was higher and endurance was lower, (2) it was prone to
being 'picked off' or 'bounced' and (3) it could be separated if the two
leading aircraft changed direction suddenly.

RAF Fighter Command Patrol Tactics

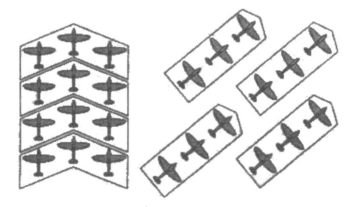

RAF 'vic' formation (on left). RAF 'vics' in line astern
(on right). In spite of its shortcomings, the tight 'vic'
formation was retained by most squadrons when patrolling
at strength during the Battle of Britain. When about to
engage enemy aircraft they often changed to the more
flexible line-astern pattern.

The Luftwaffe 'Rotte' and the sandwich manoeuvre

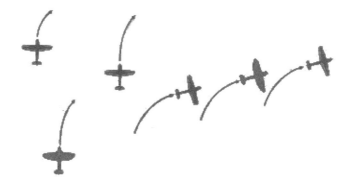

The basic Luftwaffe fighter formation consisted of two aircraft in a 'Rotte'. The leader on the left followed by the wingman, to the right and slightly behind. Both pilots had good visibility. If attacked from the rear then a 'sandwich' manoeuvre was easily executed.

The Luftwaffe 'Schwarm' of two 'Rotte'

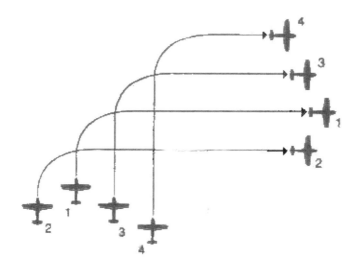

The Cross-over turn – this manoeuvre enabled the 'Schwarm' to execute a rapid turn while maintaining formation

Pictorial representation of the dog fight with Bf 109s that took place on 28 July 1940, over a convoy near Dover

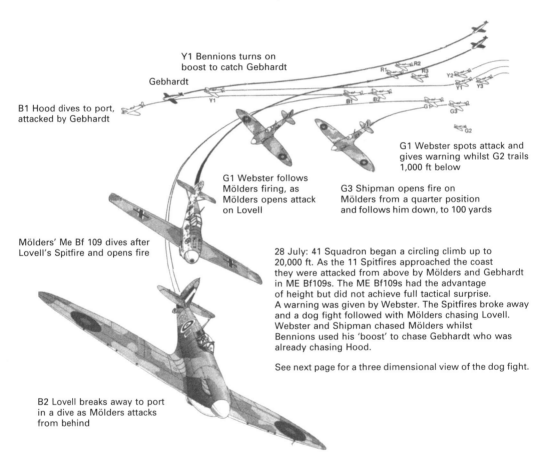

Y1 Bennions turns on boost to catch Gebhardt

Gebhardt

B1 Hood dives to port, attacked by Gebhardt

G1 Webster spots attack and gives warning whilst G2 trails 1,000 ft below

G1 Webster follows Mölders firing, as Mölders opens attack on Lovell

G3 Shipman opens fire on Mölders from a quarter position and follows him down, to 100 yards

Mölders' Me Bf 109 dives after Lovell's Spitfire and opens fire

28 July: 41 Squadron began a circling climb up to 20,000 ft. As the 11 Spitfires approached the coast they were attacked from above by Mölders and Gebhardt in ME Bf109s. The ME Bf109s had the advantage of height but did not achieve full tactical surprise. A warning was given by Webster. The Spitfires broke away and a dog fight followed with Mölders chasing Lovell. Webster and Shipman chased Mölders whilst Bennions used his 'boost' to chase Gebhardt who was already chasing Hood.

See next page for a three dimensional view of the dog fight.

B2 Lovell breaks away to port in a dive as Mölders attacks from behind

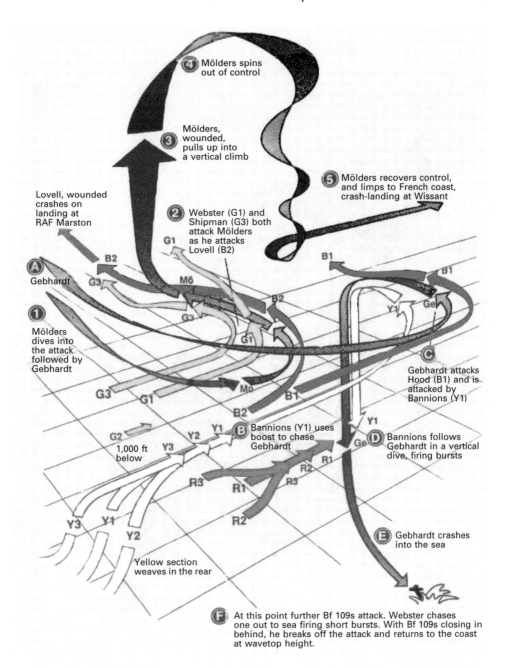

④ Mölders spins out of control

③ Mölders, wounded, pulls up into a vertical climb

⑤ Mölders recovers control, and limps to French coast, crash-landing at Wissant

Lovell, wounded crashes on landing at RAF Marston

② Webster (G1) and Shipman (G3) both attack Mölders as he attacks Lovell (B2)

Ⓐ Gebhardt

① Mölders dives into the attack followed by Gebhardt

Ⓒ Gebhardt attacks Hood (B1) and is attacked by Bannions (Y1)

Ⓑ Bannions (Y1) uses boost to chase Gebhardt

1,000 ft below

Ⓓ Bannions follows Gebhardt in a vertical dive, firing bursts

Ⓔ Gebhardt crashes into the sea

Yellow section weaves in the rear

Ⓕ At this point further Bf 109s attack. Webster chases one out to sea firing short bursts. With Bf 109s closing in behind, he breaks off the attack and returns to the coast at wavetop height.

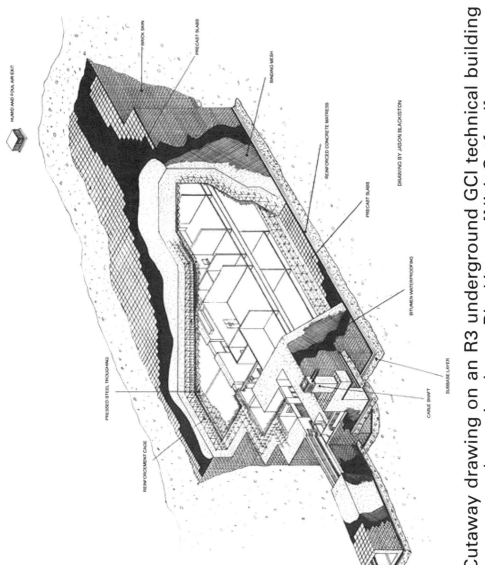

Cutaway drawing on an R3 underground GCI technical building drawn by Jason Blackiston. *[Nick Catford]*

Bibliography

Air Ministry, *The Battle of Britain August–October 1940*, HMSO
Air North, Vol. 42, No. 2, February 2002
Bickers, Richard Townshend, *The Battle of Britain*, Salamander Books
Bishop, Patrick, *Fighter Boys*, Harper Perennial
Bungay, Stephen, *The Most Dangerous Enemy*, Aurum Press
Daily Express, 23 October 1939
Doyles, Paul, *Fields of the First*, Forward Airfield Research Publishing
Goss, Chris, *Black Thursday*, Crecy Publishing
Goss, Chris, *The* Luftwaffe *Fighters' Battle of Britain*, Crecy Publishing
Goss, Chris, *The* Luftwaffe *Bombers' Battle of Britain*, Crecy Publishing
Mason, Francis, *Battle over Britain*, McWhirter Twins
Norman, Bill, Luftwaffe *over the North*, Pen and Sword
Sarker, Dilip, *Missing In Action – Resting in Peace?* Ramrod Publications
The Aeroplane magazine, 3 July 1935
The National Archives, Air 27/424
The Times Saturday Review, 14 July 1990
Wallens, R.W. 'Wally', *Flying Made My Arms Ache*, The Self-Publishing Association
Whitehead, Christopher, *The Supermarine Spitfire – an Operational History*, Delatweb International
Wood, Derek, and Dempster, Derek, *The Narrow Margin*, Hutchinson
Wynn, Kenneth G., *Men of the Battle of Britain*, Gliddon Books

Index